Jewish Ceremonial Institutions and Customs

Also from Westphalia Press
westphaliapress.org

Jewish Ceremonial Institutions and Customs

by
William Rosenau, Ph.D.

WESTPHALIA PRESS
An Imprint of Policy Studies Organization

Westphalia Press
An imprint of Policy Studies Organization
1527 New Hampshire Ave., NW
Washington, D.C. 20036
info@ipsonet.org

ISBN-13: 978-1-63391-280-9
ISBN-10: 1-63391-280-9

Cover design by Jeffrey Barnes:
jbarnesbook.design

Daniel Gutierrez-Sandoval, Executive Director
PSO and Westphalia Press

Updated material and comments on this edition
can be found at the Westphalia Press website:
www.westphaliapress.org

Seder Plate

THIS BOOK IS RESPECTFULLY INSCRIBED

BY THE AUTHOR

TO HIS FRIEND

MR. HENRY SONNEBORN

FOUNDER

OF THE

SONNEBORN COLLECTION

OF

JEWISH CEREMONIAL OBJECTS

JOHNS HOPKINS UNIVERSITY

BALTIMORE, MD.

Jewish

Ceremonial Institutions
and
Customs

by

William Rosenau, Ph. D.

Rabbi, Congregation Oheb Shalom
Associate in Post-Biblical Hebrew, Johns Hopkins University
Baltimore, Md.

Second and
Revised Edition

BALTIMORE, MD., U. S. A.
THE LORD BALTIMORE PRESS
PUBLISHERS
1912

TABLE OF CONTENTS

LIST OF ILLUSTRATIONS

PREFACE

The lectures, on which the matter contained in this volume is based, were originally delivered by me before the Oriental Seminary of the Johns Hopkins University in the winter of 1901. The reading of their abstracts in the Jewish and secular press prompted many persons to ask for the loan of my manuscript. When told that such loan could not be made, the suggestion was offered that I print the lectures for circulation. Hence, I determined to cast the lectures into popular form. The second and revised edition is published on account of the undiminished demand for this book. The accompanying plates are based on the objects of the Sonneborn collection of Jewish ceremonial objects, at the Johns Hopkins University.

W. R.

CHAPTER I

The Synagogue and its Utensils

The Jewish ceremonial institutions to be treated in the course of these chapters are such as are still in vogue among the great majority of Jews. The fact that not all Jews observe them is due to a marked tendency in the Synagogue to de-rabbinize Judaism, by laying less emphasis on the forms and more on the spirit of the faith. There is, however, not a single Jewish congregation, be the congregation ever so radical in its opposition to ritualism, in which all ceremonial institutions have been abrogated. The conviction is well nigh universal that while some institutions are absolutly meaningless for modern Jews, others are closely interwoven with the history and life of Judaism because expressive of certain distinct teachings, aims and ideals.

All Jewish ceremonial institutions do not have the same origin. Many are comparatively recent establishments; some are the creations of Talmudic times; and a few date back as far as the early days of the second Jewish commonwealth (circa 500 B. C.).

Taken in their entirety they may be grouped under two large divisions:

(1) Those obtaining in the synagogue.

(2) Those obtaining in the home.

In taking up the first class, a word or two should be said about the name, purpose, and origin of the synagogue. The term synagogue is the Greek συναγωγή, an assembly from συνάγειν "to bring together"). Its Hebrew equivalent is בית הכנסת and its Aramaic equivalent בית כנישתא "house of assembly."

Among Jews the synagogue is generally spoken of, as בית הכנסת, although the names בית תפלה "house of prayer," בית אלהים "house of God," בית יהוה "house of the Lord," מקדש "sanctuary," and בית המקדש "house of holiness," titles by which the Temple at Jerusalem was originally known, are also applied to it. The term " synagogue," by which is meant the Jewish house of worship, was coined about the middle of the third century B. C. in Alexandria, where the Jews first came in contact with Grecian culture and adopted Greek as their daily speech.

The purpose of the synagogue was always threefold: devotional, educational, and communal. While the Jew is not only not forbidden, but enjoined to indulge in private devotions at his home, and at times also at the homes of others, he is always expected to give proof of his identification with the congregation by attendance at set public services. The synagogue is considered the means for the preservation of the Jewish religion. "Do not separate thyself from the congregation"[1] is made the basis of this duty. On week days public services are conducted twice daily in the synagogue; in the morning a little after sunrise, and in the evening shortly before

[1] Aboth II, 5.

sunset. On the Sabbath and on every holiday, services are conducted on the eve of the day, in the morning, the afternoon and evening.

Every synagogue is also a school. There the young are taught the branches necessary for an active participation in the public devotion and for the proper understanding of the literature and history of Israel. In many a synagogue we may find classes for adults meeting daily for the purpose of studying the Old Testament, the Mishnah, the Talmud, the Midrashim, and later Rabbinical works. This fact accounts for the name " Schul," or " Schule," as applied to the synagogue by German Jews and Jews of German extraction.

Until recently almost every synagogue was the center of Jewish social activity. Whatever charity had to be dispensed among the deserving poor was furnished by the persons in congregational authority. In fact all communal affairs צרכי צבור were discussed and settled in the council of the synagogue.   Such is still the case in the smaller Jewish centers.

The synagogue, as a devotional, educational and communal institution is according to Talmudic tradition post-exilic in origin.   At the time of Ezra and Nehemiah, the people held gatherings for the reading of the law and the offering of prayers.   The   Temple   and   synagogue stood side by side.   בתי כנישתא תניין לבית מקדש "The synagogue is second only to the sanctuary," said an ancient teacher.[2]   In the second temple a hall known as "The hall of hewn stone" לשכת הגזית was devoted to synagogal purposes.   Already before the destruction of the second temple (70 A. C.) the synagogue grew in prominence as a social factor.   We are told in the Talmud, that synagogues flourished in all towns and villages of Palestine.   There were some even in Jerusalem.   The Palestinean synagogues mentioned as having

[2] Targum Ezek. 11 : 6.

arisen from time to time, are those of Lydda, Caesarea, Nazareth, Capernaum, and thirteen at Tiberias. The later Babylonian synagogues of which records have been preserved are those of Nehardea, Huzal, and Mata Mechasia. Celebrated synagogues known to have been located beyond Palestine and its immediate surroundings are those of Alexandria, Antioch, Damascus, Thessalonica, Ephesus, Corinth, Athens, and Rome.

The architecture of synagogues is not according to any fixed plan. All sorts of designs have been followed, the Moorish predominating and the Gothic having been carefully avoided. Israel Abrahams commenting on the architecture of the synagogue, says: " As to the shape of synagogues, no special form can be called Jewish. A famous authority of the last century maintained that no Jewish law old or new restricted the fancy of synagogue architects in this respect. He, himself, authorized the choice of an octagonal form, and this shape

is now rather popular on the continent. . . .
The Temple courts—which were used for
prayer meetings—were oblong or square,
but there was at one time a prevalent notion
in England that synagogues were round." [3]

The site chosen for the erection of synagogues is always prominent.   Synagogues
are usually built at street corners, near gate-
ways, along running streams of water, or in
open fields.   The attempt, whenever possible, is made to build synagogues on elevated
ground, in order that the house of God may
be the most conspicuous structure.   Rab, a
teacher of the third century, remarks, that
the city in which private residences tower
above the synagogue cannot escape destruction.[4]   And Rab Ashi (352-427 A. C.) believes, that the preservation of the Babylonian city Sura in times of trying persecution
must be attributed to the fact that its synagogues surpassed all other structures in size.

[3] Abrahams: "Jewish Life in the Middle Ages,"
p. 30.
[4] Sabbath 11, a.

2

A custom worthy of notice is, that a synagogue was never torn down or disposed of before another existed to take its place.

The position of the synagogue is regulated by custom. The majority of the synagogues face West and those, which do not, have their auditoriums so arranged that worshippers face the East while praying. Or, to put it in different words, the entrance is in most instances on the west side of the building and the ark toward which the worshippers turn while praying, is along the eastern wall. According to the Mishnah [5] the Jews at the time of the existence of the temple turned to the West while praying, as a protest against sun-worshippers who were in the habit of greeting the sun by turning toward it in the morning. When sun-worship ceased, about the time of the Israelitish dispersion 70 A. C., Jews living west of Jerusalem turned eastward as a mark of grief and hope, while those east of Jerusalem

[5] Succah 5: 4.

turned westward. Another reason for the existence of this custom is supposed to be found in I Kings 8 : 48.

"And (they) pray unto Thee toward their land which Thou gavest unto their fathers, the city which Thou hast chosen and the house which I have built for Thy name."

Whether synagogues need to be built so that worshippers turn toward the East is a matter of dispute among the teachers of the Talmud. Rabbi Abin declared the custom a law only while the temple existed, and Rabbis Ishmael and Oshaiah believed the custom unnecessary on the ground that God is everywhere and not confined to one spot.

Although in synagogues there is a total absence of all images, portraits and statues because of the commandment (Exodus 20 : 3, 4) :

"Thou shalt not have any other gods before Me; Thou shalt not make unto thyself any graven image, or the likeness of anything in the heavens above, the earth beneath, or the waters under the earth,"

the interior of synagogues is far from being severely plain. We often find Scriptural passages inscribed along the walls. In some instances the decorations are costly. Tradition tells of the marvelous beauty of the Alexandrian synagogue. Spanish and Italian synagogues were famous for their elaborateness. The lion is the favorite decoration. It was always regarded the symbol of protection and reminded the worshipper of Genesis 49: 9.

"Like a lion's whelp, O Judah, from the prey, my son, thou risest."

The double triangle מגן דוד "The shield of David," although visible on the exterior and interior of almost every synagogue, is anything but of Jewish origin.[9]

Israel Abrahams remarks: "Some authorities applied the restriction (namely of decorating synagogues with images) only to the human figure. . . . Others forbade all representation of natural objects. . . . In the twelfth century the Cologne synagogue had painted glass windows and it was not an

[9] Friedlander's "Jewish Religion"; Jewish Encycl. Vol. VIII, p. 251.

unknown thing for birds and snakes, proba-
bly grotesques, rather than accurate repre-
sentations, to appear without Rabbinical
sanction on the walls of the synagogue." [1]

In the majority of synagogues we find no
musical instruments. Wherever the organ
exists it is a comparatively recent institution.
The reason for the absence of instrumental
music lies in the prohibition to play instruments on Sabbaths and Holy days [9] (as such
playing is considered work) and in the desire to preserve an apparent mourning for
the destruction of the temple.

Only a small proportion of synagogues
can boast of family pews. In most of them
the women are separated from the men; the
latter congregating in the so-called " court
for men " עזרת אנשים, and the former in the
so-called " court for women " עזרת נשים. To
the court for men women are not admitted.
The court for women is, as a rule, a room
adjoining the court for men, the two courts

[1] Abrahams, Jewish Life in the Middle Ages, p. 29.
[9] Erubin 104, a.

communicating by a window or balcony. If there is no separate apartment for women, the women are given seats behind the men and are curtained off from the latter. It is in this way that the women are enabled to follow the services. Galleries, like those in modern synagogues where family pews have not yet been introduced, were not known in earlier times. The separation of the sexes undoubtedly dates back to the עזרת נשים " the court for women " in the Temple.⁹ The reasons urged at present for the exclusion of women from the main auditorium of some synagogues are, the Biblical precedent that women were not permitted to enter the premises of the sanctuary and the fear that their presence might distract the attention of the men in their devotions. Israel Abrahams tells, that formerly, in their own prayer meetings, the women were led by female precentors, some of whom acquired enviable reputations as such. The epitaph

⁹ Middoth 2: 5.

of one of them, Urania of Worms, belong-
ing perhaps to the thirteenth century, runs
thus:

"This headstone commemorates the eminent and
excellent lady Urania, the daughter of R. Abraham,
who was the chief of the synagogue singers.   His
prayer for his people rose up unto glory.

And as to her, she, too, with sweet tunefulness
officiated before the female worshippers to whom she
sang the hymnal portions.   In devout service her
memory shall be preserved." [10]

The seats for the worshippers are in many
instances arranged along the walls of the
synagogue in order to leave the center of the
auditorium perfectly free for the pulpit.   In
such instances the seats of the learned of the
congregation are nearest to the eastern wall
or immediately in front of the ark.

As a rule the auditorium consists of three
parts corresponding to the three apartments
of the temple of Jerusalem.   The first apartment, as one enters the door of the auditorium, corresponding to the temple court, is
the space occupied by the congregation dur-

[10] "Jewish Life in the Middle Ages," p. 26.

ing worship. The second apartment, corresponding to the inner space of the temple,
where altar, shew bread, table, and candelabra were found, consists of a platform with
the שולחן (lit. " table ") " reading desk." In
the Talmud this platform is called " bema "
(from the Greek βῆμα). It is known also by
the name " almemar " corrupted from the
Arabic " al-minbar," pulpit. The third
apartment, corresponding to the " Holy of
Holies " in the temple with the ark of the
covenant in which were deposited the two
tablets of stone, consists of the ark with the
scrolls of the law. The third apartment is
separated from the second by a " curtain "
פרכת.

There is nothing in the first apartment,
the space occupied by the congregation, re-
quiring special description.

The second apartment, " bema," or " almemar," is a raised platform. The officiating precentor, known as שליח צבור " messenger of the congregation " to the Most High,
here conducts the services and reads the sec-

tions from the law and the prophets. It is
also the place where all public announcements are made. In conducting the services
the appointed readers in orthodox synagogues always face the East and hence have
their backs turned to the congregation. The
reading desk, also called כורסיא, is always
decorated with a richly embroidered cover.
In some synagogues the foundation of the
bema extends several inches below the floor
of the auditorium, in order that the following passage may be literally observed:

"Out of the depths have I cried unto the Lord." [11]

If the bema is not built thus, special
prayers directed to God are delivered from
a place lower than the bema, usually the
place between the bema and the ark.

In many synagogues there is no space
between the bema and the ark—the bema
being pushed forward toward the ark. Maimonides, a teacher of the twelfth century,
fixes the bema in the center of the auditor-

[11] Ps. 130: 1.

ium, as located in the ancient Alexandrian
synagogue, in order that the precentor might
be heard equally well in all parts of the
building. Joseph Caro, a teacher of the sixteenth century and author of the Shulchan
Aruch, " the prepared table " (a code on the
Jewish ritual, to which frequent references
will be made), grants the privilege of mov-
ing the bema toward the ark. In Germany,
Austria, England, France and America,
Jews have built synagogues availing themselves of the privilege granted by Joseph
Caro, while in Portugal and Spain the opinion of Maimonides is followed.

Between the bema and the ark, that is,
immediately in front of the ark, we find suspended the נר תמיד " perpetual lamp." It is,
as its name indicates, kept constantly burning. It is made of gold, silver or burnished
brass. As an institution of the synagogue
it is of comparatively recent establishment.
It is not mentioned by Rabbinical teachers.
Its Biblical authority is:

"And thou shalt command the children of Israel
that they bring the pure olive oil beaten out for the
lighting to cause the lamp to burn always. In the
tabernacle of the congregation without the veil
which is before the testimony Aaron and his sons
shall order it from evening to morning before the
Lord. It shall be a statute forever unto their generations, on behalf of the children of Israel." [12]

Symbolically it is the representation of the
conviction of Jews, that the light of instruction issues from the synagogue.

The ark, called תבה or ארון or הקודש רון,
and occupying the middle of the east side of
every synagogue, is constructed of either
wood or marble. In earlier times it was
simply a niche in the wall. It is the reposi-
tory for the scrolls, of which in all congregations there are almost always several.
Some congregations are known to own between thirty and forty. The ark is always
approached by steps leading to it from the
second apartment. On the top of every ark
are found two tablets, with the first two
words of each of the ten commandments in
Hebrew characters, representative of the two

[12] Ex. 27 : 20, 21.

tablets of stone brought by Moses from Mt.
Sinai. Immediately below these tablets the
inscription   דע לפני מי אתה עומד   " Know before Whom thou art standing," is seen in
many synagogues. The whole ark, or sometimes only the receptacle for the scrolls, is
covered by a curtain, beautifully embroidered. This curtain is made either of satin,
silk or velvet. A favorite figure on the curtain is a crown with the letters כ׳ת the initials of כתר תורה " The crown of the law "
below it. An inscription often found on the
curtain is : שויתי יהוה לנגדי תמיד " I have always
set the Lord before me." [13] On different occasions we find different-colored curtains.
The curtain of the ark, for the most part,
corresponds in color with the cover of the
reader's desk and with the robes of the
scrolls. If, for example, red prevails on
Sabbaths, purple is used on Passover, Feast
of Weeks and Feast of Booths. White is,
however, everywhere the color of the vest-

[13] Ps. 16: 8.

Parocheth—Curtain for Ark

ments on the New Year's festival and the Day of Atonement.

Formerly, the ark was portable, like the ark of the covenant. On certain extraordinary occasions, when on account of absence of rain a general fast was ordered, the ark with the scrolls was carried into the street, where special services were conducted.

The scrolls found in the ark contain the five books of Moses in Hebrew characters. The text is unpointed and unpunctuated; that is, only the consonants are given. Neither are chapters and verses indicated. Every scroll is known as a " sefer," " book " or as " torah," " law " or as " sefer torah," " the book of the law."

The special rules governing the making of the scrolls are given in Caro's Shulchan Aruch." The sefer torah, or scroll, is a parchment roll written by hand upon the thoroughly cured skin of a clean animal. The skin of the calf or sheep is usually taken

" Yoreh Deah, Sefer Torah, §§270-284.

for this purpose, though the skin of other animals may be used. The ink is made of lamp-black. While the text is unpointed and unpunctuated the paragraphs are marked according to the Masora, some starting a new line, others leaving space at the end of the line. The width of a leaf, often consisting of several columns, must not exceed the circumference of the scroll when closed. The width of the margin alongside of the separate columns is regulated by law. The separate leaves, when completed, are fastened together with the sinews of a clean animal, so as to form a scroll, and are then mounted on wooden rollers, the handles of which, protruding above and below, are of either wood, ivory or silver. The writer, "sopher," must have his attention riveted upon his work. The parchment must be written upon one side only. When a leaf has been completed the writing must always be turned upward. If dust gathers on the written parchment it is regarded a mark of disrespect shown the law. Mistakes may be

corrected, but no mistakes should be left un-
corrected for more than thirty days.   The
person writing a scroll must be not only an
expert scribe but also a man of unquestioned
piety.

When the scroll is in the ark it is attired
as follows: First it is held secure by a linen,
silk, or velvet wrapper usually inscribed.   A
silver clasp is sometimes used.   The linen,
silk, and velvet wrappers are in some localities the donations of the male children and
are by them brought to the synagogue on
the occasion of their first visit to the house
of God.   This first visit usually takes place
as soon as possible after circumcision.   The
child is taken to the synagogue and there it
places the wrapper on the scrolls.   In this
event the wrapper contains the full names of
the child and of its parents in Hebrew characters.   When the scroll is secure a robe is
placed over it.   Robes are of different colors,
mostly corresponding to the color of the curtain suspended in front of the ark, and are
beautifully embroidered in gold.   Some of

the inscriptions embroidered on the robes
are:

תורת יהוה תמימה   " The law of the Lord is
is perfect."

מצות יהוה ברה " The commandment of the
Lord is clear."

סומך צדיקים יהוה " The support of the righteous is the Lord."

כ׳ת meaning כתר תורה " The crown of the
law."

Sometimes we find only the double triangle, the so-called shield of David.

In addition to the robe many a scroll
is handsomely decorated with trimmings,
known as כלי קודש " holy vessels " made of
metal. These vessels are in most instances
of silver. Over the upper rollers are placed
artistically worked top pieces with bells.
Over the robe an elaborate breast plate is
suspended by a chain. And over the breast
plate a pointer extends, terminating in the
figure of a hand, and hence called " yad "
(hand), with which the reader points to the
text while reciting the Pentateuchal portion.

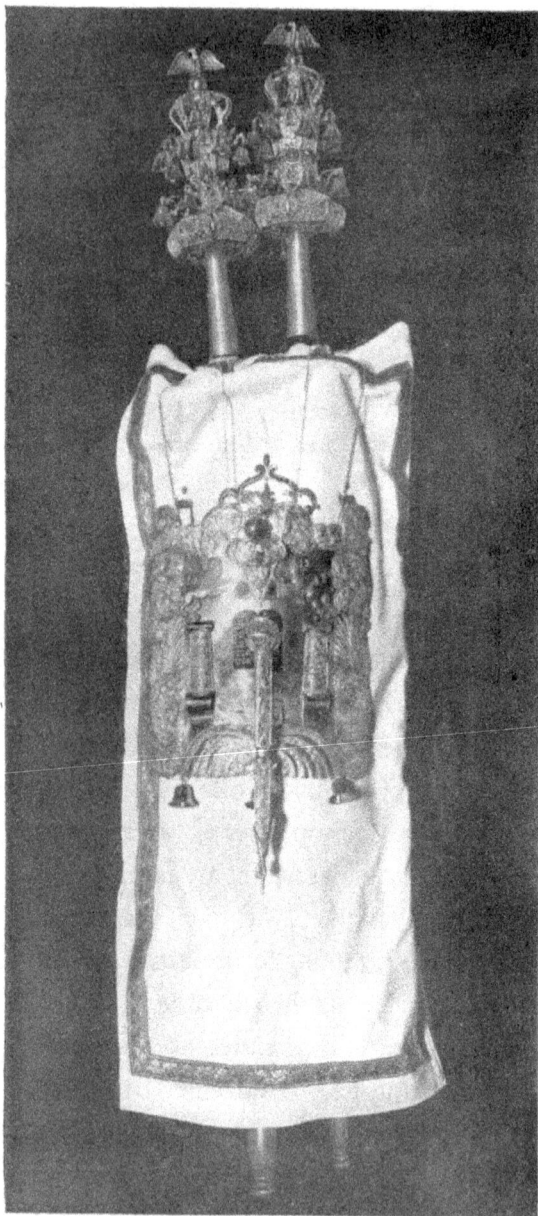

Torah with Robe and Ornaments

1 Silver Shield for Torah   2 Silver Pointer   3-4 Silver Ornaments for the Upper Part of Torah

This pointer is suspended from the scroll by
a chain and is often twelve inches long. A
fact worth mentioning is that the top pieces
for the rollers and the breast plate are usually decorated at the upper end with a
crown emblematic of the crown of the law.
In addition to the crown decorating the
breast plate, are also the figures of lions—
symbols of strength.

The scroll is read every Sabbath, usually
between the morning service " shacharith "
and the additional or forenoon service
" mussaf."

The recitation of the portion from the
scrolls is called " the reading of the law,"
קריאת התורה.   The reading of the law once
every seven years we find enjoined in Deut.
31 : 10-13.

" At the end of every seven years, in the solemnity of the year of release, in the Feast of Tabernacles
when all Israel is come to appear before the Lord
thy God, in the place which He shall choose, thou
shalt read the law before all Israel in their hearing.
Gather the people together, men, women and children, and the stranger that is within thy gates, that
they may hear, and that they may learn, and fear the

Lord your God, and observe to do all the words of
this law; and that their children, which have not
known anything, may hear and learn to fear the Lord
your God."

For the purpose of Sabbath readings the
Pentateuch is divided into a large number
of sections. There are twelve in Genesis,
eleven in Exodus, ten in Leviticus, ten in
Numbers and eleven in Deuteronomy; or
fifty-four in all. In a year of 12 lunar
months, consisting of either 353, 354 or 355
days, there are at the most 51 Sabbaths. To
get over the entire law in one year in such
congregations, in which the annual cycle
prevails, the combination of two consecutive
sections into one takes place on some Sabbaths. The reading of the law is conducted
in regular order beginning with the first
chapter of Genesis, on the Sabbath immediately following the Festival of Rejoicing
Over the Law, celebrated on the 23d day of
Tishri. In order not to bring the law to an
end at any time, the first chapter of Genesis
is read on the Feast of Rejoicing Over the
Law as soon as the book of Deuteronomy

has been completed.   The sections are known
by names taken from one word or two
words in their respective opening verses.
Thus the first one is known as " Bereshith "
(in the beginning), the second as " Noah,"
the third as " Lech Lecha " (get thee out),
and so on.   On holidays the portions of the
law read are usually those which contain
some direct or indirect reference to the occasion celebrated.   If a holiday happens to fall
on Sabbath, the regular Sabbath portion is
set aside for the holiday section.   On Sabbaths occurring on the new moon, on the
four Sabbaths immediately preceding Passover, and on holidays two scrolls are usually
read.   From the first the Sabbath or holiday
section is read, while from the second an
account of the special Biblical custom attaching to the specific occasion in question is
read.   Each section is called a sidra (order),
and each sidra is divided into seven sub-sections.   When the scroll is put on the desk
eight males are called to the bema.   Every

one of these recites the following blessing before the reading of a sub-section:

" Praise ye the Lord, Who is to be praised; praised
be the Lord, Who is to be praised forever and aye."

" Praised be the Lord, our God, King of the
Universe, Who has chosen us from among all nations
and has given us His law.   Praised be Thou, O
Lord, Giver of the law."

Upon the completion of the sub-section the
person called to the scroll recites this second
benediction:

" Praised be the Lord, our God, King of the
Universe, Who has given us a law of truth and has
placed within us the longing for life eternal. Praised
be Thou, O Lord, Giver of the law."

Originally every person called to the desk
read his own sub-section.   Later, however,
in order not to embarrass persons unable to
read the unpointed text, the precentor or
reader, appointed for the purpose (בעל קורא)
read the whole sidra.   The only exception
made was the occasion of a boy's Bar Mitzvah, confirmation (an event which commemorates the attainment of his thirteenth
birthday), when the boy himself reads his
portion.   The order in which people are

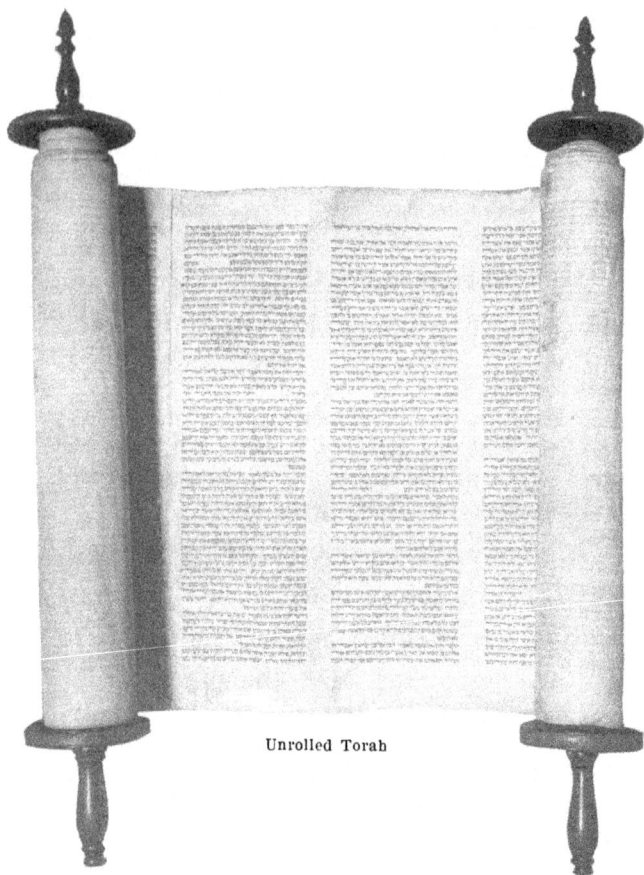

Unrolled Torah

called to the desk is as follows: First we
have a representative of the priestly family
of Aaron called a Cohen; then a descendant
of the house of Levi, called Levi; and then
six others, supposed to belong to the other
tribes of Israel, who are simply termed
Israelites. The six, known as Israelites, are
summoned to the desk as the third, the
fourth, the fifth, the sixth, the seventh and
Maftir "he who is to conclude." Among
Portuguese Jews, as in many orthodox
European and Asiatic synagogues, those
called to the desk are summoned by their full
Hebrew names. In earlier times this custom
obtained among all Jews.

The eighth person summoned (Maftir),
whose Pentateuchal sub-section consists of
the last few verses of the seventh sub-section, is obliged to read the portion from the
Prophets assigned for the Sabbath. A prophetical section is read on every Sabbath and
holiday. The subject matter of the prophetical section selected by the liturgists of the
synagogue always treats a theme similar to

the one discussed in the Pentateuchal portion. The origin of the Haphtaroth, prophetical sections, is a matter of dispute. One theory holds, that they originated in times of persecution, when Jews were forbidden to read the scroll. Another claims, that the Haphtaroth served as a protest against the Samaritans, who regarded only the Torah and not the other Scriptural writings holy. It is, however, more than likely that these prophetical sections were introduced as soon as the prophetical writings became a part of the Biblical canon.

The scroll is also read during the services on Sabbath afternoon (the section then always consisting of the opening sub-section of the portion of the following Sabbath), and on Mondays and Thursdays at the early morning service. The reading of the scroll on Mondays and Thursdays is supposed to have originated at the time of Ezra, who provided for such reading for the benefit of the country people. They came to the city on these days and could not, on account of the Sabbath law, which prevented their travelling great distances, come to listen to the reading of the regular portion on the Sabbath day.

In some congregations, instead of an annual cycle of the reading of the Pentateuch, a three years' cycle, and in others even a seven years' cycle obtains. The great majority of congregations, however, still adhere to the annual cycle.

The calling of persons to the desk for the recitation of benedictions over a sub-section has been discontinued by many congregations in order to maintain decorum during services, which was often materially impaired. In such cases the regularly officiating precentor is the only one to recite the benedictions.

It should be stated here that the number of persons called to the bema in those congregations where the annual cycle obtains is 3 on Sabbath afternoons and week days; 4 on new moon and half holidays (Chol Hammoed), by which is meant the festive

week of Passover and Feast of Booths; 5
on festivals; and 6 on the Day of Atonement. These numbers given for holidays
and the Day of Atonement do not include
the Maftir, the concluding section accompanied by a prophetical portion, added on
these days, as has been before stated.

The manner of the reading of the law is
worthy of explanation. The section is usually sung. This is also the case in the reading of the Haphtarah, though the intona-
tion of the Haphtarah is different from that
of the sections of the scrolls. The accents
found in the Masoretic text of the Bible,
serve as musical notes to indicate how certain words are to be intoned. The Greek
word $\tau\rho o\pi\acute{\eta}$ (Trope) is the name given by
German Jews to the peculiar chant, while
the Hebrew " Neginah " (melody) is used
in the same sense among Portuguese Jews.
This chant has been developed into an
elaborate system. Among the so-called Reform Jews, the chant is not used in the reading of the Scriptures. Nor is the chant the

same for all occasions and among all Jews.
The chant for the New Year and Day of
Atonement is different from that of the Sabbath, and that of German Jews from that of
the Portuguese Jews. The custom of chanting the Bible is undoubtedly as old as the
use of the Scriptures in the devotion of the
synagogue. A Talmudical authority remarks:

" Whoever reads the Bible without pleasantness (i. e., modulation of the voice or
chanting) and teaches the oral law without
song, to him are applied the words taken
from Ezekiel 20 : 25 : ' I also gave them
statutes which were not good.' " [15]

The removal of the scrolls from the ark
before reading and their return to the ark
after reading is accompanied with great
solemnity. The character of the service is
not always the same the world over. Jews
located in sections widely separated from
one another have different ritualistic forms

[15] Megillah 29, b.

of procedure.   The one most common in Europe and America is given here.   First a hymn of glorification is rendered, opening: " There is none among the gods like Thee, O Lord."   The congregation rises while the ark is opened and the precentor steps before the ark reciting the words: " When the ark journeyed, Moses said: Arise, O Lord, and let Thine enemies be scattered and let those who hate Thee flee before Thee. From Zion the law goes forth and the word of the Lord from Jerusalem.   Praised be He, who gave the law in its holiness to Israel, His people."   Then follow the declaration of the oneness of God and the proclamation of His greatness.   From the ark the precentor goes in solemn procession with the scroll to the bema, where the ornaments, robe and wrapper are removed, and the scroll is prepared for reading.   Before the reading takes place the scroll is unrolled to the extent of a few columns of the text and lifted up before the assembled congregation as in

Portuguese congregations while the precentor exclaims:

" This is the law which Moses put before the children of Israel by command of the Lord."

The honor of closing and dressing the scrolls is in most congregations conferred upon two worshippers, the one holding, while the other re-invests the scroll with wrapper, robe and ornaments.

When the scroll is returned to the ark songs of praise are again rendered, which conclude with the following exclamations:

" Valuable instruction I have given you. Forsake ye not my law. It is a tree of life to those who lay hold of it, and its supporters are happy. Its ways are ways of pleasantness, and all its paths are peace. Cause us, O Lord, to return to Thee and we shall return. Renew our days as of old."

CHAPTER II

In our attempt to become acquainted with
the religious customs and practices of Israel
we shall in this chapter make in thought a
visit to the Jewish house of worship and observe some of the special institutions worthy
of note. There is perhaps no class of people
to whom the house of worship is more sacred
than to the Jew. The laws preventing its
desecration are numerous and are framed to
meet all violations of sanctity, in which men
may indulge. The Jewish teachers of the
second century placed the same emphasis
upon respect for the synagogue as upon
regard for the ancient temple, of which
the synagogue is the substitute. They forbade laughing and talking within its walls.[1]
At his entrance and departure the worship-

[1] Megillah 28, a.

per is, as they said, to conduct himself with decorum. They tell that one should go quickly to the house of God, but leave it slowly.[2] Eating and drinking are prohibited in the synagogue.[3] Refuge from the heat and rain was not to be taken in it.[4] People are admonished to be among the first at its services.[5] Before entering the synagogue the hands should be washed. For this purpose a pitcher with water is found in the ante-room, corresponding to the laver before the sanctuary and temple. In some localities burial from the synagogue is forbidden because of the defilement of the holy place by the corpse. An exception is made only in case the dead is one learned in the law.

Upon close examination we find that a public service is never begun unless the quorum fixed by tradition is present. This quorum consists of ten men. Less than ten

[2] Sabbath 32, a.
[3] Megillah 28, a.
[4] Megillah 28, b.
[5] Baba Metzia 107, a.

men is never regarded a congregation suffi-
ciently large for public devotion.   In the
Ethics of the Fathers we read

"If ten are assembled and are engaged in the study
of the law, the Shechinah resides among them."[6]

It is on the basis of this opinion that the
size of the quorum was fixed.   While ten
constituted a quorum in the earliest days of
the existence of the synagogue, Treatise
Soferim mentions that in Palestine services
were once held with seven men.[7]   Women
do not count as members of the quorum.
The Rabbinical law exempts women from
the performance of all religious duties which
are to be executed at a definite time.[8]   However, in some instances of the modern occidental synagogue, not only women are
counted in the congregational quorum, but
also ten people are not considered absolutely
necessary for holding public worship.

Many communities are in the habit of
having ten persons attend services at a

[6] Aboth 3: 4.
[7] Soferim 10: 7.
[8] Kiddushin 1: 7.

compensation, in order that the conducting of a service be not prevented. During the Middle Ages, when in all probability this custom arose,[9] the persons engaged for this purpose were the older students of the Talmudic schools. Later, however, it became customary to select persons from the deserving poor.

While in the synagogue, worshippers keep their heads covered, a practice observed also by many persons when reading any and every Hebrew text, because literature written in the so-called "holy tongue" is considered specially sacred and its study is regarded a religious act. A not insignificant number of Jews consider it a sacrilege to go with uncovered head at any time. There is no Biblical warrant for this custom, although it is often stated, that as the high priest wore a head covering when officiating in the sanctuary, so should every Jew when praying. The wearing of the head gear is undoubtedly

[9] Abrahams: "Jewish Life in the Middle Ages," p. 57.

nothing more than a remnant of orientalism. Among Mohammedans and Parsees the same practice obtains. Nor does the lengthy discussion of the Talmudical passage לא יקל את ראשו כנגד שער המזרח " One should not make his head light before the Eastern gate " [10] convince the student that the wearing of the hat is anything more than a custom without basis in law.

If some people consider the wearing of a head-covering an important feature in the devotion of the Jew, the cause is none other than the insistence of Paul of Tarsus, that men should sit in the church with uncovered head as the surest means of severing their connection with the synagogue. Says Paul:

"Every man praying or prophesying, having his head covered, dishonoreth his head. For a man indeed ought not to cover his head." [11] [12]

---

[10] Berachoth 54, a.

[11] I Cor. 2: 4, 7.

[12] For an exhaustive treatise of this custom in all its various aspects we refer to Fluegel's "Gedanken ueber Religioese Braeuche und Anschauungen."

In a number of Jewish congregations the head covering is removed during worship on the ground that occidental residence and oriental habits are incompatible. This is no new departure. Israel Abrahams tells, that on the Feast of Rejoicing Over the Law boys in the 15th century ascended the bema bare-headed during the reading of the Pentateuchal section.[13] Even adults were known to have prayed bare-headed in France.[14]

A point noteworthy in this connection is, that as the head is to be kept covered the hands are to be kept uncovered. Gloves must therefore be removed during devotion. This custom is based on the synonymous use of praying with the Biblical phrase " spreading forth the hands."

During the early morning prayers on week days, but not on Sabbaths and holidays, in the Jew's private as well as public devotions, males over thirteen years of age

[13] Abrahams: " Jewish Life in the Middle Ages," p. 32.
[14] Geiger: Juedische Zeitschrift, III, 142.

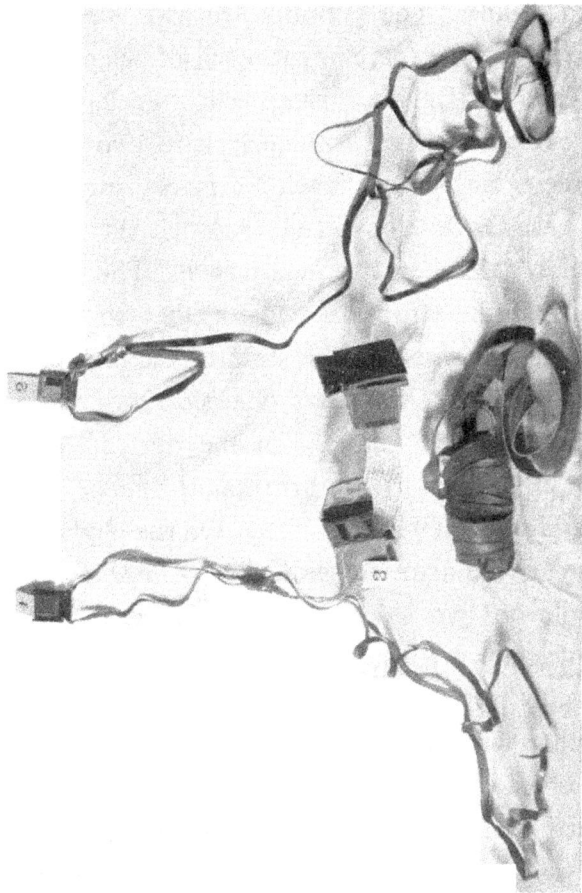

1 Phylactery for Head   2 Phylactery for Arm   3 Rabbenu Tam's Phylacteries

wear Tefillin (phylacteries), on the left arm
and head. The Tefillin are two square
boxes of hard parchment, each of which is
called a " Bayith," receptacle, varying in
size from half of a cubic inch to two and
three cubic inches. Each receptacle rests on
a base with a protruding loop, through
which a leather strap is drawn. The two
ends of the strap are tied together so that
the knot formed by the strap of the phylactery for the head has the shape of the
Hebrew letter " daleth " ד and the knot of
the phylactery of the arm has the shape of
the Hebrew letter " yad " י. On the phylactery of the arm we see no letter impressed,
while on two sides of the exterior of the
phylactery of the head we see the letter
" shin " ש embossed. This " shin," together with the " daleth " and " yad," just
referred to, constitute the word שדי (" shaddai ") " Almighty." The interior of the
phylactery for the head is divided into four
compartments. Into each one of these is
put a piece of parchment containing one of

the four sections of the Pentateuch, inter-
preted as commanding the wearing of the
phylacteries.   The parchment put into the
first compartment, starting with the right
side as worn on the head, contains the following:

"And the Lord spoke unto Moses saying, Sanctify
unto me all the first born, whatsoever openeth the
womb among the children of Israel, both of man and
of beast: it is mine.

And Moses said unto the people, Remember this
day in which ye came out from Egypt, out of the
house of bondage; for by strength of hand the Lord
brought you out from this place; there shall no
leavened bread be eaten.

This day came ye out in the month of Abib.

And it shall be when the Lord shall bring thee into
the land of the Canaanites, and the Hittites, and the
Amorites, and the Hivites, and the Jebusites, which
he sware unto thy fathers to give thee, a land flow-
ing with milk and honey, that thou shalt keep this
service in this month.

Seven days thou shalt eat unleavened bread, and in
the seventh day shall be a feast to the Lord.

Unleavened bread shall be eaten seven days, and
there shall no leavened bread be seen with thee,
neither shall there be leaven seen with thee in all thy
quarters.

And thou shalt shew thy son in that day, saying,
This is done because of that which the Lord did unto
me when I came forth out of Egypt.

And it shall be for a sign unto thee upon thine hand, and for a memorial between thine eyes, that the Lord's law may be in thy mouth; for with a strong hand hath the Lord brought thee out of Egypt.

Thou shalt therefore keep this ordinance in his season from year to year." [15]

The second compartment contains these passages:

"And it shall be when the Lord shall bring thee into the land of the Canaanites, as he sware unto thee and unto thy fathers and shall give it thee.

That thou shalt set apart unto the Lord all that openeth the matrix and every firstling that cometh of a beast which thou hast; the male shall be the Lord's.

And every firstling of an ass thou shalt redeem with a lamb; and if thou wilt not redeem it then thou shalt break his neck; and all the first born of man among thy children shalt thou redeem.

And it shall be when thy son asketh thee in time to come saying, What is this? that thou shalt say unto him, By strength of hand the Lord brought us out from Egypt, from the house of bondage;

And it came to pass when Pharaoh would hardly let us go, that the Lord slew all the first born in the land of Egypt, both the first born of man and the first born of beasts; therefore I sacrifice to the Lord all that openeth the matrix being males; but all the first born of my children I redeem.

And it shall be for a token upon thine hand and for frontlets between thine eyes; for by strength of hand the Lord brought us forth out of Egypt." [16]

---

[15] Ex. 13: 1-10.   [16] Ex. 13: 11-16.

In the third compartment are the words:

"Hear, O Israel, the Lord, our God, is one Lord.

And thou shalt love the Lord, thy God, with all thine heart, and with all thy soul, and with all thy might.

And these words which I command thee this day shall be in thine heart;

And thou shalt teach them diligently unto thy children, and shalt talk of them when thou sittest in thine house, and when thou walkest by the way, and when thou liest down, and when thou risest up.

And thou shalt bind them for a sign upon thine hand, and they shall be as frontlets between thine eyes.

And thou shalt write them upon the posts of thy house and on thy gates."[17]

The parchment in the fourth compartment reads:

"And it shall come to pass if ye shall harken diligently unto my commandments, which I command you this day, to love the Lord, your God, and to serve Him with all your heart and with all your soul,

That I will give you the rain of your land in his due season; the first rain and the latter rain, that thou mayest gather in thy corn, and thy wine, and thine oil.

And I will send grass in thy fields for thy cattle, that thou mayest eat and be full.

Take heed to yourselves that your heart be not deceived and ye turn aside and serve other gods, and worship them;

---

[17] Deut. 6: 4-9.

And then the Lord's wrath be kindled against you, and He shut up the heaven that there be no rain, and that the land yield not her fruit; and lest ye perish quickly from off the good land which the Lord giveth you.

Therefore shall ye lay up these, my words, in your heart and in your soul, and bind them for a sign upon your hand, that they may be as frontlets between your eyes.

And ye shall teach them, your children, speaking of them when thou sittest in thine house, and when thou walkest by the way, when thou liest down and when thou risest up.

And thou shalt write them upon the door-posts of thine house and upon thy gates." [18]

The interior of the phylactery for the hand consists of only one compartment, into which is put a parchment containing the above four sections written continuously. The materials used in the making of the phylacteries must be of the skin of clean animals and the sections indicated must be written according to the rules governing the writing of the scrolls. The Talmudists trace every feature of the phylacteries, certainly without foundation, as far back as Moses, as they do almost every other cere-

[18] Deut. 11: 13-20.

monial institution known to them. Although
the straps of the phylacteries are usually of
black leather, the use of black leather could
not have been universal, as one Rabbi [19] is
said to have fastened his phylacteries with
purple ribbons. The Biblical passage, taken
as the legal basis of the phylacteries, is the
repeated Pentateuchal command, " and thou
shalt bind them for a sign upon thy hand,
and they shall be as frontlets between thine
eyes." This Biblical command is, in all probability, not to be taken literally, but figura-
tively. It, very likely, means to cherish and
remember the words of the Lord.

In putting the phylacteries on the body
the phylactery of the arm is taken first.
The box is fixed firmly on the naked left
arm, upon the biceps muscle, above the elbow,
and while this is done the worshipper recites
the benediction:

"Praised be the Lord, our God, King of the
Universe, Who has sanctified us with His commandments and commanded us to lay the phylacteries."

---

[19] Menachoth 34-36.

Then the strap is wound seven times about the arm below the elbow. Thereupon the phylactery for the head is put on with the box placed in the middle of the forehead below the hair and the two straps are arranged to hang over the shoulders, one on each side. While putting on this phylactery this benediction is recited:

"Praised be the Lord, our God, King of the Universe, Who has sanctified us with His commandments and enjoined upon us the commandment of the phylactery."

Returning to the phylactery of the hand, its strap is wound three times about the middle finger and then around the whole hand. While this is done the following words are recited:

"I betroth thee unto me forever; I betroth thee unto me in righteousness, in judgment, in kindness and in mercy. I betroth thee unto me in faithfulness and thou shalt know the Lord." [20]

The worshipper now petitions God to consider the performance of the commandment regarding the phylacteries, as though all six

[20] Hosea 2: 21, 22.

hundred and thirteen commandments had
been faithfully executed. Here follows the
devotion.

When the devotion is ended the phylacteries are usually removed, that of the head
being taken first. In putting them aside the
straps are twisted around the base of the
phylacteries. The phylacteries, when not in
use, are kept as a rule in a bag of velvet or
silk, beautifully embroidered with the shield
of David, or otherwise ornamented. While
to-day phylacteries are worn by most Jews,
only during their morning devotion, some
people formerly wore them all day. There
are some persons who lay two kinds of phylacteries; those of Rashi, a teacher of the
12th century, in whose phylacteries the Biblical sections of the parchment are written in
the order stated above, and those of Rashi's
grandson, Rabbi Jacob, known as Rabbenu
Tam, who held that the inverse of the order
given by Rashi, should be the order of the
Biblical sections on the parchments. The
Karaites, a sect established in the eighth

century by Anan Ben David denying the authority of Rabbinical tradition and adhering only to the Bible, do not lay phylacteries. Among many Jews of to-day they have also fallen into disuse.

The term " Tefillin " reminds one of " tefillah," prayer, and hence denotes things used during prayer. Originally it may have meant ornament. It is a substitute for the Biblical (totafah) " frontlet." Its English equivalent, phylacteries, is derived from the Greek $\varphi v\lambda\alpha\varkappa\tau\eta\rho\iota\alpha$ not because they serve, like the $\varphi v\lambda\alpha\varkappa\tau\eta\rho\iota\alpha$, as amulets, but because the tefillin resemble the phylacteria in external appearance. Placed on arm and head they are to serve as reminders to cherish with the heart and to contemplate with the mind the law of God.

During the morning service every male adult wears also a (talith) praying scarf. The reader wears the talith on all occasions. In some congregations mourners wear it during the benediction in which they extol God's wisdom and greatness. On the Fast

of Ab in commemoration of the destruction
of Jerusalem, the talith is put on before the
afternoon service in place of being put on
at the beginning of the morning service.
Among the Portuguese Jews even boys wear
a talith. Some people have two praying
scarfs, one for week days and another of bet-
ter material for Sabbaths and holidays. It
usually constitutes one of the remembrances
given a boy on the occasion of his thirteenth
birthday, the time of his religious majority.

The talith is a rectangular piece of linen,
wool, or silk cloth. Some teachers objected
to the linen praying scarf. The talith
usually has blue or black stripes near its corners running all the way across the material
and is decorated with a crown (atarah), consisting of a silk ribbon or a strip of either
silver or gold passementerie, running along
the exterior upper part, so that when put on
the " crown " fits around the neck. If the
crown is of silver or gold it must be the pure
metal and should be marked so. On each of
the four corners of the talith are fringes—

1 Large Talith
2 Fringe for Talith
3 Atarah—Silver Collar for Talith

linen fringes for the linen talith, silk fringes for the silk talith, and woolen fringes for the woolen talith. Silk, wool and linen dare not be mixed, the mixture of various materials being forbidden by Biblical law.[21] Should they be mixed the praying shawl is unfit for ritualistic use. These fringes are attached in obedience to the following Biblical injunction:

"Speak unto the children of Israel and bid them that they make them fringes in the borders of their garments, throughout their generations, and that they put upon the fringe of their borders a cord of blue; and it shall be unto you for a fringe that you may look upon it and remember all the commandments of the Lord and do them; and that ye seek not after your own heart and your own eyes after which ye go astray."[22]

Another passage supposed to enjoin the use of the talith is:

"Thou shalt make for thyself fringes upon the four corners of your garments with which thou coverest thyself."[23]

---

[21] Lev. 19: 19; Deut. 22: 11.
[22] Numb. 15: 38, 39.
[23] Deut. 22: 12.

In view of the fact that the exact shade of
the prescribed purple cord in the fringe cannot be procured, white is used exclusively.
Already in Talmudic times, about the fifth
century of the Christian era, white was substituted for the purple cord, owing to the
difficulties of procuring the proper shade of
purple.   The material for the fringes must
be manufactured for their express purpose.
If of wool, they must be of wool carefully
shorn, and not plucked from the sheep.   The
fringes must be spun by Jews.   They may be
spun by non-Jews, only provided a Jew
supervises the work.   These fringes are put
in a hole about an inch from the edge of the
talith.   The manner of their attachment is
the following: Four threads, one of which
is longer than the others, are passed through
the hole; the two parts of the threads are
bound together by the longer thread in a
double knot; then the longer part of the
longer thread is wound seven times about the
seven halves of the four threads; then follow
eight windings, then eleven, and then thir-

teen windings, and after each set of windings two knots are made. According to the
Kabbalah, these knots and windings have a
secret meaning. The windings, thirty-nine
in all, correspond to the numerical value of
the letters constituting the two words אחד
יהוה " The Lord is One," since each letter of
the Hebrew alphabet has numerical significance.

The talith is worn either carefully folded
over the shoulders, open and hanging over
the back, or often over the head. When put
on the worshipper recites:

"Praised be the Lord, our God, King of the
Universe, Who has sanctified us with His commandments, and commanded us to encircle ourselves with
fringes."

The merit attached to wearing the fringes
is considered very great, as great as that of
laying the phylacteries. The talith, when
folded, is usually stored away in a beautiful
bag made for the purpose. The bag is of
either silk or velvet and elaborately decorated.

In distinction to the talith " gadol," the
large praying scarf, used during public devotions, there is the smaller praying scarf
with fringes, used by all males, young boys
included.   It is known also by the name of
" arba kanfoth," the four cornered garment.
It consists of any piece of cloth with an
aperture in the center large enough to allow
the head to pass through, so that half of it
falls over and rests on the back, while the
other half falls over and rests on the chest.
It is usually worn below the outer garments
and is put on in the morning, immediately
after washing.   When put on, this benediction is recited :

" Praised be the Lord, our God, King of the
Universe, Who has sanctified us with His commandments and enjoined upon us the command with regard to the fringes."

The " arba kanfoth " is not removed again
until the wearer retires for the night.   The
small praying scarf undoubtedly originated
at the time of persecution, when Jews were

Small Talith

obliged to practice their ceremonies secretly. Like the phylacteries the praying scarf has fallen into disuse among some Jews.

CHAPTER III

The Sabbath Service

From institutions characteristic of the week-day services let us proceed to those marking the Sabbath. The Jewish Sabbath and holy days do not begin with midnight, but with sundown of the day preceding, and end with the following sundown. This custom is based on the oft-recurring phrase in the Biblical creation story, " It was evening, and it was morning " (the evening always preceding the morning in the mention of the day). In many synagogues the Sabbath is not welcomed in any other way than by special hymns and songs. However, into a great number of synagogues a ceremony called the " Kiddush," a feature of the Sabbath sanctification in the Jewish home, has found its way. The " Kiddush " consists of the lifting up of a cup of wine by the precentor at the close of the

evening devotion. In doing this the precentor praises God the Creator of the Universe (Who is reported to have rested on
the seventh day), for the creation of the fruit
of the vine and for the institution of the Sabbath. The " Kiddush " runs as follows:

"And it was evening and it was morning the sixth
day.

And the heavens and earth were finished and all
their hosts. And on the seventh day God had finished His work which He had made, and He rested
on the seventh day from all His work which He had
made. And God blessed the seventh day and hallowed it, because He rested thereon from all His
work which God had created and made. Blessed be
the Lord, our God, King of the Universe, Who creates the fruit of the vine.

"Blessed be the Lord, our God, King of the
Universe, Who has sanctified us by His commandments, and has taken pleasure in us, and in love and
favor has given us His holy Sabbath as an inherit-
ance, a memorial of the creation, that day being also
the first of the holy convocations in remembrance of
the departure from Egypt, for Thou hast chosen us,
and sanctified us above all nations and in love and
favor hast given us Thy holy Sabbath as an inherit-
ance. Blessed be the Lord, Who hallows the
Sabbath."

Having concluded his benedictions the
precentor does not drink from the cup, but

places the cup upon the reading desk to be
handed around among the boys attending
the services.   The sanctification of the day
with wine takes place, on the eve of all
sacred days except on fast days, in congregations where the sanctification (Kiddush)
has become a fixed institution.   Although
according to the Talmud[1] the " Kiddush "
belonged to the evening meal in the home,
אין קדוש אלא במקום סעודה the institution found
its way into the public devotion of the synagogue.   According to the teachers of the
third century the synagogue was the lodging
place for strangers.   For this purpose separate apartments were fitted up.   In order to
sanctify the day with the proper joy, " for
it is the wine which rejoiceth the heart of
man," the Kiddush was instituted at the
close of the evening service, more especially
since wine was no doubt not served at the
free meals with which strangers were supplied.   Although the House of Worship is

---

[1] Pesachim 101, a.

no longer devoted to giving strangers lodging, the Kiddush has nevertheless been retained in many synagogues.

As the Sabbath is welcomed with a special institution in the synagogue, so it is concluded after sunset on Saturday upon the appearance of three stars in the horizon. This concluding institution bears the name " Habdalah," separation, distinction. The " Habdalah " has been preserved in all synagogues, the members of which believe in strict adherence to the Sabbath law as laid down by the Rabbis. It is the signal to the worshipper that he may again attend to work as indicated in the Rabbinical maxim,

אסור לו לאדם שיעשה חפציו קודם שיבדיל

" Man is forbidden to attend to his needs until he has conformed to the 'Habdalah.' " [2]

Originally the " Habdalah " consisted of the interpolation of a special benediction in the body of the evening service, but later its present form was added.

[2] Sabbath 150, a.

1 and 2 Spice Boxes for Habdalah   :: Candlestick for Habdalah

The " Habdalah " is conducted as follows: Wine is poured into a goblet until it overflows into the saucer beneath. The goblet is then lifted up by the precentor with his right hand. At the same time he holds in his left hand a box containing sweet smelling spices, while the sexton or some young boy in attendance at the services holds a burning taper. The reader begins the ceremony by intoning the words:

"Behold, God is my salvation. I will trust and not be afraid, for the Lord, Yah, is my strength and my song. He is also become my salvation, and ye shall draw water with joy from the fountains of salvation. Salvation is with the Lord. May Thy blessing be on Thy people. Selah. The Lord of Hosts is with us. The God of Jacob is our refuge. Selah. The Jews were once favored with delight and joy, gladness and honor. Thus may it also be with us. I will take the cup of salvation and call upon the name of the Lord."

Hereupon follows the benediction over the goblet of wine:

"Blessed be the Lord, our God, King of the Universe, Creator of the fruit of the vine."

Putting down again the goblet the precentor recites the benediction over the spices. It reads:

"Blessed be the Lord, our God, King of the Universe, Who creates diverse species of spices."

Opening the box and inhaling some of the fragrance the precentor proceeds to the blessing over the light. He holds his hands over the burning taper and says:

"Blessed be the Lord, our God, King of the Universe, Who creates the light of the fire."

Taking the burning taper from him who has held it, the precentor extinguishes it with the wine, which is in the saucer, and while doing so says:

"Blessed be the Lord, our God, King of the Universe, Who has made a distinction between things sacred and profane, between light and darkness, between Israel and other nations, between the seventh day and the six days of labor. Blessed be the Lord, Who has made distinction between things sacred and profane."

The various elements of the Habdalah are not without their symbolical significance. The principal meal of the day was taken after sundown. Light and burning incense marked its special character. These could not be procured on the Sabbath, on which the use of fire was prohibited in the words:

" Ye shall not kindle a fire in your dwellings," [3] and therefore had to be enjoyed upon
the conclusion of the Sabbath.   To-day the
spice, the substitute for the incense, is according to some teachers made to stand for
the pleasure which the Sabbath brings, while
the light is to remind one of God's creation
on the first day, to which the approaching
day of the week corresponds. The overflow-
ing of the cup with wine is symbolical of the
dispensation of God's unbounded grace for
which the Jew hopes. The placing of the
hands over the light by the precentor, when
he reaches the words " Between light and
darkness," is simply to illustrate the words
by showing the light inside of the hands and
the shadow outside of them.

The Habdalah is also celebrated at the
conclusion of holidays, but with this difference, that the blessing of God as Creator of
the light is omitted, since on holidays, excepting the Day of Atonement, fire could be

[3] Ex. 35 : 3.

handled. On the night of the Day of Atonement the blessing over the spices is omitted
from the Habdalah, unless the Day of
Atonement happens to occur on a Sabbath,
in which case all four blessings are recited.
The Habdalah undergoes a change also if
the Sabbath is followed by the ninth day of
Ab, a fast day in commemoration of the destruction of Jerusalem. In this event only
the blessing over the light is pronounced on
Saturday night, that of the spices is omitted,
and the remaining two blessings are recited
Sunday after the fast.

The goblets used, both in the sanctification and the conclusion of the Sabbath, are
of different material and of various designs.
The more costly one is always used for the
sanctification. The goblets are in the shape
of either cups or tumblers. If the goblet is
of silver, it is as a rule engraved with
Hebrew characters.

The spice boxes used at the conclusion of
the Sabbath also differ both in material and
design. A popular box is one made of cedar

wood said to be imported from the Lebanon. Boxes of this kind are usually inscribed with the Hebrew for " Jerusalem." If the box consists of silver it is usually in the form of a tower with a silver flag flying on the top. Spice boxes range in size from three to twelve inches. The collection of Jewish ceremonial objects at the Smithsonian Institution at the United States National Museum in Washington contains a spice bottle made of china with its neck in oxidized silver. The taper used is always of pure wax. It consists either of one piece or three pieces twisted together. It is used either with or without a candlestick, but mostly without one. It must be kindled by none but the observing Jew, who is forbidden to touch fire on the Sabbath. In addition to these two institutions there are no others marking the services on the Sabbath in the synagogue. We shall now treat the institutions marking the public services on holy days and festive seasons.

CHAPTER IV

The ceremonial institutions marking the observance of Jewish holidays in the synagogue proper constitute the subject matter of this and the next chapter. The occasion engaging our attention first is " Pesach," Passover, as it is the first festival celebrated in the order of the Jewish calendar months. Before proceeding to a description of its peculiar public observances, a word on the Jewish religious calendar is not only in order, but also necessary. I call the calendar religious, because in matters non-religious, or secular, that mode of reckoning obtains among Jews which their non-Jewish neighbors follow.

The Jewish calendar is the lunar calendar. Every month consists of either 29 or 30 days, and is regulated by the revolution of the moon around the earth. New moon always indicates the beginning of the new month. The ordinary year consists of twelve lunar months, making 353, 354, or 355 days in all. Noting from this difference between the lunar year and the solar year of 365 days, that in a very short time holidays would be shifted very far from their appointed season, the question arises, in what way is this difficulty offset? Seven times in every cycle of 19 years, as in the Metonic calendar, provision is made for a leap year, by the addition of a thirteenth month. The leap years are the third, sixth, eighth, eleventh, fourteenth, seventeenth and nineteenth of every cycle of nineteen years. The names of the months, which are of Babylonian origin, a fact to which the Talmud testifies, are Nisan, Iyar, Sivan, Tammuz, Ab, Ellul, Tishri, Heshvan, Kislev, Tebeth, Shebat, Adar, while the name of the thirteenth month in case of leap year is Adar Sheni, second Adar. The first month, Nisan, occurs in spring and begins in either March or April. Nisan is made the first month because in this month the exode from

Egypt, marking the beginning of Israel's national life, took place. The Jewish calendar is so arranged that the first day of the seventh month, Tishri, cannot fall on Sunday, Wednesday or Friday (in order to prevent the Day of Atonement from occurring on Friday or Sunday, because the preparation of food is forbidden on the Sabbath), and to prevent the last day of the Feast of Booths from happening on Saturday. Whenever the beginning of Tishri threatens to fall on Sunday, Wednesday or Friday a day is added to the passing year and taken from the immediately following one.

In the earliest times great difficulty attached to the observance of holidays on the same day by all Jews, but the difficulty was easily met. The new moon had to be proclaimed by the Synhedrin. As soon as two witnesses testified before this august body to the appearance of the new moon and their testimony was found to be based on fact, the people living in Palestine, Syria and Baby-

lonia were notified of the new moon, either
by messengers or fire signals given on top
of hills. If no witnesses were found to tes-
tify, the day, on which the new moon was
expected, was added to the preceding month.
The celebration of festivals depended altogether upon the proclamation of the new
moon by the Synhedrin. There were, however, communities, whom word could not
reach in time for the observance of the
month's beginning, which was celebrated as
a half holiday. In order to effect simultane-
ity of observance among all Jews, those living too far from the seat of the Synhedrin
to be informed in time, celebrated not only
two days as the beginning of the month,
namely, the last day of the passing month
and the first day of the coming month, but
also two days of the festive seasons, on
which, according to Scriptures, a holy convocation was ordered. Rosh Hashanah
(the first day of the 7th month, the day of
Memorial) was observed even by Palestinean Jews for two days, while the Day of

Atonement was observed everywhere for only one day, owing to the strain which fasting produced on the human body. In the great majority of congregations the celebration of holidays for two days is still continued although unnecessary since the formation of an exact calendar. Jews have been in possession of a correctly computed calendar since the middle of the fourth century, the work of Hillel II, or Hillel the younger, as he is commonly called.

In order not to neglect the observance of days commanded by Jewish law every member of the synagogue, as a rule, provides himself with a calendar every year. The Hebrew equivalent for calendar is " Luach," which originally denotes " table " or " tablet." These calendars contain not only the Hebrew dates and the corresponding secular dates, but also indicate festivals and holy seasons, and the sections read from the scrolls in the synagogue on the various Sabbaths of the year.

But to return to (Pesach) Passover! It
is the holiday celebrated from the eve of the
15th of Nisan (either March or April) for
seven days among some Jews, and for eight
days among most of them, in commemoration of the deliverance of ancient Israel from
Egyptian slavery. It is known by the name
" Feast of unleavened bread," because of the
absence of all leaven from Jewish homes
and the use of only the unleavened as enjoined in Exodus 12 : 15 ; 13 : 7 ; and other
passages. Only the first and seventh days
are according to Scriptures holy convocations, while the rest are half holidays, although, as indicated in the discussion of the
Jewish calendar, the second and the additional eighth days are dignified as full holidays. According to the Shulchan Aruch, the
work of Joseph Caro, referred to before, no
mourning addresses are to be delivered during the whole month of Nisan, on account of
the joy which should mark the celebration
of Israel's emancipation from slavery. All
fasting was also interdicted, with the excep-

tion of the fast enjoined upon the first born males on the day preceding Passover, in commemoration of the fact, that the first born Israelites were spared the 10th plague which befell Egypt. If the eve of Passover happens to fall on Saturday the first born fasts on Thursday preceding.

Passover is more of a family feast, if the number of ceremonial institutions determines its character. In the synagogue proper there are very few special features to be observed in addition to the reading of psalms of thanksgiving and glorification, incorporated into the regular service or taking the place of a part of it. During the forenoon, in the additional service of the first day of Passover, which follows immediately upon the return of the scrolls to the ark, the prayer for rain recited during the entire autumn and winter, beginning with the " Feast of Assembly " to be spoken of later, is discontinued, and the prayer for dew is inserted in its place. The reading of these prayers is, as may be readily seen, based

altogether upon Palestinean climatic conditions, and hardly upon conditions obtaining
in other countries.

A custom worthy of note, which is begun
immediately after the evening service on
the eve of the second day of Passover, and
continued until the Feast of Weeks, namely
for 50 days, is the counting of the Omer.
An Omer is a measure about the size of a
half of a gallon. It contained the first fruit
brought by the ancient Israelites as an offering to the priest, when, as pilgrims, they
came to Jerusalem on this feast. The institution of counting is based on the following:

"And ye shall count unto you from the morrow,
after the Sabbath, from the day that ye brought the
sheaf of the wave offering, seven Sabbaths shall ye
complete; even unto the morrow, after the seventh
Sabbath, shall ye number fifty days."[1]

The counting is preceded by a blessing,
which reads:

"Blessed be the Lord . . . Who has sanctified us
by His commandments, and has commanded us to
count the days of the Omer."

---

[1] Lev. 23: 15, 16.

The manner of counting is as follows:
" This day is the —— day since the Omer."

After seven days the number of weeks in
the Omer is also specified. The days of
counting are called the " Sefirah." During
this time Jews do not marry or give ban-
quets, as it is a season replete with sad
memories. Massacres of Jews took place
at this time during both the reign of the
Emperor Hadrian and the Crusades. The
33d day of the Omer, the 18th of Iyar, is,
however, excepted. Joyous occasions may
be celebrated at this time, as according to
tradition a plague which raged among the
disciples of Rabbi Akibah (135 B. C.), was
on that day stayed. In some congregations
a tablet is suspended from the wall of the
synagogue indicating the exact day of the
Omer season.

Before closing the subject of Passover it
should be stated that on it the " Song of
Songs " is read, owing to the verse: " Behold the winter is gone."[2]

[2] Can. 2: 15.

Whereas this verse calls attention to the passing of winter, the book of Canticles, as a whole, is regarded a love song fittingly commemorating and symbolizing the betrothal of Israel to God.

On the 6th day of the 3d month, called Sivan, occurring either in May or June, Jews celebrate a feast, which according to Deuteronomy [3] is called " Feast of Weeks," because occurring at the expiration of seven full weeks after the second day of Passover. In Lev. 23 : 16 it is identified with the 50th day of the counting of the Omer. It is according to Ex. 23 : 16, the Feast of the early harvest gathered in Palestine, on which day the offering of the first fruit had to be brought to Jerusalem. This custom of bringing the offering of the first fruit has been replaced in many an occidental synagogue by decorating the Jewish house of worship with trees, plants, and flowers. The Feast of Weeks is known also by the name " Day of the Giving of the Law," because

[3] Deut. 16: 10.

of an existing tradition to the effect that the revelation of God's word to Israel at Mount Sinai took place on the 6th day of the 3d month. Often termed the marriage anniversary of Israel to God, a great portion of the modern European and American Synagogue has selected this day as the time, on which young men and women are confirmed, or formally accepted as active members of their faith. In addition to selected holiday prayers and chants the day is not celebrated by distinct ceremonies. The Biblical scroll read on this festival is the book of Ruth, because it tells of Ruth's acceptance of the true faith and the harvest of the first fruits in the fields of Boaz.

In many congregations, the night preceding the Feast of Weeks is observed in the school rooms of the synagogue by a watch, during which, passages from the scriptures and Talmudical books are recited. This institution has its origin in the three days' preparation which was enjoined upon an-

cient Israel.[4]   A similar watch is held the
7th night of the Feast of Tabernacles, to be
explained later.   The watch in most cases
includes a repast.   During the middle ages
the Feast of Weeks was the occasion, on
which every male child at 5 years of age
and at a later age, if physically weak, was introduced to school life.   He was given his
first lesson in Hebrew, and in the synagogue
was offered the opportunity of hearing the
ten commandments read from the scroll,
which constitutes a part of the day's scriptural section.[5]

On the 17th of the fourth month, Tammuz, a fast day is observed in the synagogues conforming to Rabbinical law, in
commemoration of the breach made in the
wall of Jerusalem.   Another fast is celebrated on the 9th of the fifth month, Ab, in
memory of the destruction of both the first
and second Temples.   During the three
weeks intervening between these two fasts,

[4] Ex. 19: 10-12.
[5] Jewish Life in Middle Ages, p. 348.

many Jews abstain from pleasure and the use
of meat in their diet. Some impose this
restriction upon themselves only during the
eight days immediately preceding the 9th of
Ab. The fast of Tammuz, like all other
fasts, except the Day of Atonement, com-
mences at daybreak, but the fast of Ab lasts,
like the Day of Atonement, for twenty-four
hours, from evening until evening. The
restrictions, which the Jew puts on himself
on these occasions, are endured as a mark
of his mourning over the downfall of the
holy city. These two fasts are ignored in a
number of synagogues, because their con-
stituents view the downfall of Jerusalem as
an opportunity given to Israel to fulfil its
mission, although the memory of Jerusalem
is cherished by all Jews. During the day
of these two fasts various elegies are recited.
On the fast of Ab, the book of Lamentations
is the scroll designated for reading in the
synagogue.

We may here mention some of the other
fasts, observed by a great many Jews, and

the reasons for their celebration. They are
the Fast of Gedaliah on the third day of the
seventh month, Tishri (celebrated on account of the murder of Gedaliah, Governor
of Jerusalem); the Fast of Tebeth, on the
tenth day of the tenth month, Tebeth (in
memory of the commencement of the siege
of Jerusalem); and the Fast of Esther, on
the thirteenth day of the twelfth month,
Adar, or in case of leap year the thirteenth
day of the thirteenth month, Adar Sheni
(in commemoration of the contemplated
slaughter of the Jews of Persia).

CHAPTER V

THE TISHRI HOLIDAYS AND THE HALF HOLIDAYS

We now approach the study of the most important days for modern Jews. They are those from the first to the tenth day of the seventh month, Tishri. Taken together they are known as " Yamim Noraim," solemn days, and " Asereth Y'me Teshubah," ten days of Penitence. Their purpose is to prompt the Jew to self-examination and to reconciliation with God. The first of these days is called " Rosh Hashanah," New Year—a name the Biblical writers do not know. In the Bible [1] it is termed " Yom Teruah," day of blowing the alarm, and " Zichron Teruah," memorial of blowing the alarm. The terms " Day of Memorial " and " Day of Judgment " are also applied to this day. It is not our purpose here to explain

[1] Numb. 29: 1.

how the first of the seventh month instead of
the first day of the first month served as the
beginning of the New Year. Suffice it to
say, that the first of Tishri was in many
respects the commencement of the year. In
this month the Jubilee year began, slaves
were emancipated and landed property re-
verted to its original owner.

The most prominent feature in the public devotion of the synagogue consists of the
blowing of the ram's horn. Long before the
arrival of the festival its notes are heard.
The whole of the preceding month (Ellul)
is regarded a month of preparation. " Seli-
choth," special prayers for forgiveness of
sin and the blowing of the Shofar mark the
preparation. This month of preparation
takes its character from a well-known tradition. It is reported, that on the first of Ellul
Moses ascended Mt. Sinai for the third time
and returned on the tenth of Tishri, with the
assurance of God's pardon to Israel. While
in Biblica¹ times the Shofar was used for all
sorts of announcements, like that of New

Moon and festivals, the year of release, the call to battle, as signal of victory, and as an instrument in processions, its purpose on this holiday is to rouse Jews to the serious contemplation of their sinfulness and their duty to lead a godly life. Saadya, a teacher of the tenth century, holds, that the Shofar reminds Jews of the creation, their duty to God, the revelation on Mt. Sinai, the teachings of the prophets, the destruction of the Temple, the binding of Isaac as a sacrifice, imminent danger, the Day of Judgment, the redemption of Israel, and the resurrection.

The Shofar is made of a ram's horn flattened by heat. It is always crooked and is finished with a mouth-piece. It is absolutely devoid of all decorations.

The Shofar is blown for the first time on New Year before the scrolls are returned to the ark and is preceded by the following benedictions:

"Blessed be the Lord, our God, King of the Universe, Who has sanctified us with His commandments, and commanded us to hear the sound of the Shofar.

"Blessed be the Lord, our God, King of the Universe, Who has kept us alive, sustained us and caused us to enjoy this season."

There are four kinds of sounds produced by the Shofar:

(a) Tekiah—the unbroken sound.

(b) Shebarim—the broken sound.

(c) Teruah—the wave-like sound.

(d) The long Tekiah—the prolonged unbroken sound.

These four sounds are arranged in three sets of blasts.

The first is Tekiah, Shebarim, Teruah; sounded three times in succession.

The second is Tekiah, Shebarim, Tekiah; also sounded three times in succession.

The third is Tekiah, Teruah, Tekiah; sounded three times, with this exception, that the last Tekiah is the prolonged Tekiah.

After every set of blasts a pause follows, during which devotional reflections are recited. The first of these sets of blasts is directed to the angel Sharshia, the second to the angel Tartiel, and after the third set all angels are implored to help worshippers to

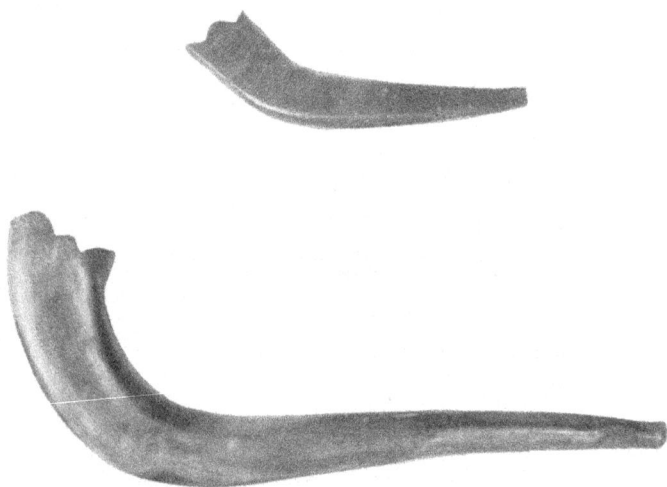

Different Sizes of Shofar (Ram's Horn)

become thoroughly imbued with the meaning of the Shofar's sounds. The doctrine
with regard to these angels was introduced
by the Kabbalists and is not Jewish.

In the Mussaf services, the service following the return of the scrolls to the ark, there
are again three sets of blasts with prayers
intervening between the first and second, and
the second and third sets of blasts. If the
first day of the New Year occurs on the Sabbath the Shofar is not sounded, owing to the
labor it entails. The blowing then takes
place only on the second day. In some congregations, where New Year is celebrated
for one day only, the ritual provides for the
blowing of the Shofar, even on Sabbath.[2]

The person blowing the Shofar must perform this service standing on the bema of
the synagogue. The Shofar when blown is
held in the right hand, with the opening,
from which the sound issues, turned upward. In addition to the month of Ellul
and New Year, the Shofar is sounded at the

[2] Szold-Jastrow Ritual.

close of the Day of Atonement. Among the Portuguese Jews it is then sounded four times, and among others but once. And finally it is sounded on the seventh day of the Feast of Tabernacles, at each of the seven circuits made around the synagogue.

One word more about the Jewish New Year. On New Year, as well as on the subsequent holy day, the worshippers, in the most conservative synagogues, wear their burial shrouds as an incentive to sincere repentance, for it helps to remind people of their mortality and the uncertainty of life.

In addition to fasting, the special confessions of guilt, and the petitions for forgiveness, there is but one peculiar ceremonial institution marking the observance of the Day of Atonement. The institution referred to consists of the kindling of a large wax taper by every member of the congregation near the bema of the synagogue or at the seats of worshippers in memory of departed dear ones. The taper is always large enough to burn the entire twenty-four hours of the fast. The reason for the kindling of the taper lies in the comparison the Bible makes between the soul of man, in the immortality of which the Jew believes, and a lamp or light.

We now proceed to the consideration of the Feast of Booths occurring on the fifteenth day of the seventh month, Tishri. It is observed for seven days, the first day alone being a holy convocation, while the remaining six days are half holidays. It is instituted in memory of the dwelling of the children of Israel in booths when they journeyed through the wilderness.[3] Being a harvest festival, the Feast of Booths is observed in the synagogue by songs of praise, the decoration of the synagogue with plants and fruits, more especially by the use of " the palm branch," " Lulab " and the " citron," " Ethrog." The preparation of the palm branch is based on the passage :

" And ye shall take unto you on the first day the fruit of the goodly tree, branches of palm trees, and

---

[3] Lev. 23 : 43.

boughs of thick leaved trees, and willows of the
brook, and ye shall rejoice before the Lord your God
seven days." [4]

The palm branch is decorated at the
lower part with myrtle and willow branches,
attached to the palm branch by means of
leaves of the palm tree. When the palm
branch and citron are picked up the benediction recited is:

"Blessed be the Lord, our God, King of the
Universe, Who has sanctified us with His commandments and commanded us the use of the palm
branch."

On the first day is added the benediction,
in which God is thanked for having spared
the worshipper to enjoy this season. Not
only the precentor but many a layman is
provided with a lulab and ethrog. The palm
branch and the citron are lifted up in full
view of the congregation during the rendition
of psalms of praise and the recitation of a
prayer for God's redemption, taking place
while a circuit is made around the synagogue.
On Sabbath the lulab is not taken up, as the

[4] Lev. 23 : 40.

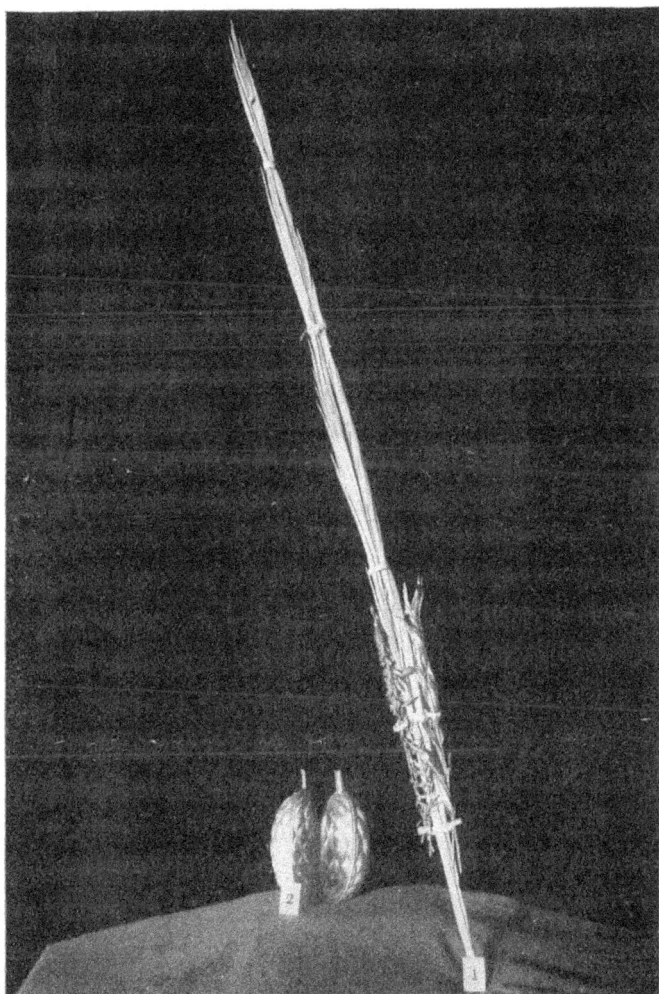

1 Palm Branch   2 Citron Receptacle (Silver)

carrying of it is regarded a form of work, desecrating the day. The Karaites do not give the lulab a place in the synagogal service, but believe that it is to be used in the building of the " Succah," Booth.

In some synagogues a booth is erected, similar to that met in the Jewish home. We shall not speak of the booth in this connection, as its discussion has its proper place among the ceremonial institutions, characterizing the Jewish home, to be taken up later.

The last day of the Feast of Booths is called " Hoshana Rabba," because on this day numerous petitions for the salvation of Israel are recited. During the intoning of these petitions, the worshippers make seven circuits around the auditorium of the synagogue. Among Portuguese Jews the Shofar is sounded on this day, as if to give those, who have not become thoroughly reconciled with God on the Atonement Day, a last opportunity of repentance before the final judgment of God is sealed. It is on the eve of this festival that a watch takes place, similar to the one held on the eve of the Feast of Weeks.

On " Shemini Atzereth," the Feast of Assembly, celebrated on the 22d day of the seventh month, Tishri, no special ceremonial institution, except the reading of the scroll of Ecclesiastes, marks the public service. The day following, however, the 23d day of the seventh month, known as " Simchath Torah," " Feast of Rejoicing Over the Law," is characterized by an elaborate institution. The feast is post-Biblical in origin and was not a fixed institution until the annual cycle of Pentateuchal reading from the scrolls was firmly established. As has been mentioned in the first chapter, the last section of Deuteronomy is read on this day from one scroll and the first section of Genesis from another. The privileges of reciting the customary benedictions over the last sub-section, read from the first scroll, and over the first sub-section, read from the second, are prized as precious privileges and hence eagerly sought. The two persons who procure these privileges, often at the expense of rich offerings to the congregational treasury, are respectively titled " Chasan Torah," Bridegroom of the Law, and " Chasan Bereshith," Bridegroom of Genesis. In many congregations, where this day is still observed, these two Bridegrooms often tender their fellow worshippers a repast. On the Day of Rejoicing Over the Law special inducements are held out to the younger members of the congregation to participate actively in the public service. Carrying flags with burning tapers, young boys will, on the eve of the day, join the procession in which all the scrolls owned by the congregation are carried around the auditorium of the synagogue. As the procession moves through the auditorium women throw nuts and raisins from the galleries on the men and boys marching below. While the scrolls are out of the ark a burning taper is usually put into it. In some communities it is customary to call even young boys, who

have not yet attained the age of religious
majority, to the bema to recite the benedictions over a sub-section of the Pentateuchal
festive portion.

Beginning with the 25th day of the ninth
month, Kislev, Jews celebrate for eight
days " Chanukkah," Feast of Dedication, in
commemoration of the defeat of Antiochus
Epiphanes and the re-dedication of the
Temple at Jerusalem by Judas Maccabeus
(164 B. C.). It is called also " Feast of the
Asmoneans." It is celebrated by kindling
on every evening of the feast, beginning
with the eve of the first day, wax tapers or
lamps. On the eve of the first day one
light is kindled. The number of lights
steadily increases until the eighth day is
reached, the number always corresponding
to the ordinal number of the day celebrated.
A separate taper is used for the kindling of
the lights and bears the name " Shammash,"
servant. In the Talmud there is a discussion as to whether the number of lights
should increase or decrease from day to day.

Hillel believes in the increase and Shammai in the decrease. For the kindling of such tapers every congregation possesses a candelabrum made either of burnished brass or silver. The ceremony of kindling lights is based on a tradition, which tells that when the Temple was cleansed by Judas Maccabeus of all debris, he found a cruse of oil, hermetically closed with the high priest's seal, the size of which indicated that there would be sufficient oil in it to last merely for a day, whereas it miraculously lasted for eight days. On lighting the Chanukkah lights the following benedictions are recited:

"Praised be the Lord, our God, King of the Universe, Who has sanctified us with His commandments and has commanded us to kindle the lights of Chanukkah."

"Praised be the Lord, our God, King of the Universe, Who wrought miracles for our fathers in days of old at this season."

On the first night a third benediction, consisting of thanks to God for having spared the worshipper in health and life, is added.

After the lighting of the tapers or lamps, a hymn of praise is sung, dwelling upon the frequent intercession of God's help in the time of Israel's early oppression.

Purim, rendered according to Biblical etymology " Feast of Lots," and celebrated on the 14th day of the twelfth month, Adar, and in case of leap year on the 14th day of the thirteenth month, has its public service in the synagogue marked by the reading of the book of Esther both on the eve and morning of the holiday.

The book of Esther is not read on this occasion from an ordinary text of the Old Testament, but from a parchment scroll, which is called " Megillah," the scroll.

The Megillah must be carefully written on the skin of a clean animal, by a Jewish Scribe, with good ink, and not printed, although printed copies are in existence and are used by members of the congregation, while following the reading of the precentor, who invariably has before him a parchment scroll.   The names of the Sons of

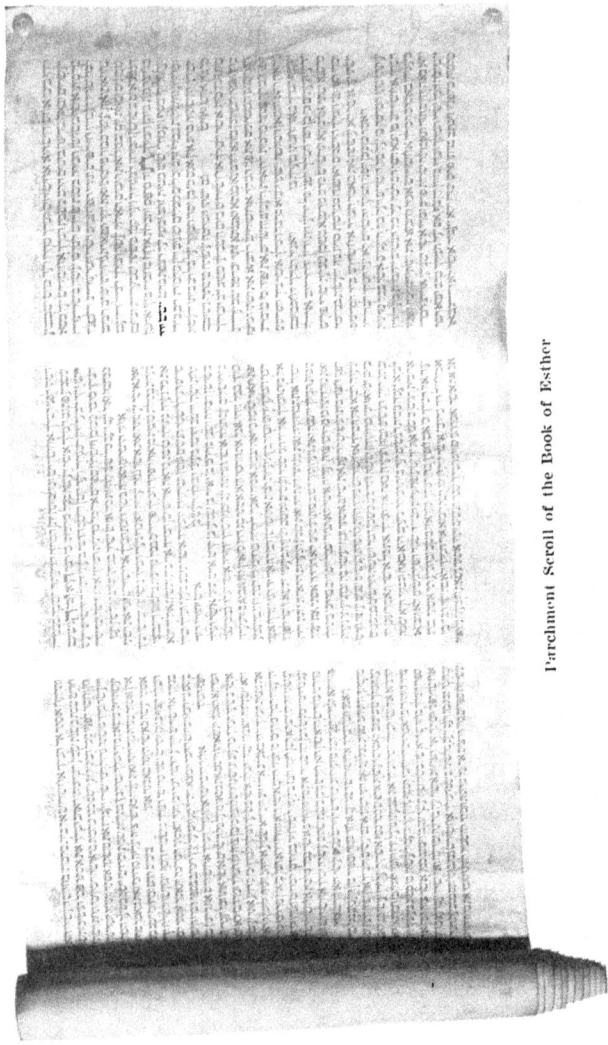

Parchment Scroll of the Book of Esther

Haman must be written on separate lines, one below the other.

The book of Esther is chanted in a melody unlike that characterizing the reading of the scrolls of the law or the selections from the prophets. The recitation of Esther by heart is forbidden, however well acquainted the precentor may be with the book. The precentor is compelled to have the text before him. While everybody is in duty bound to read the book of Esther for himself, persons not understanding Hebrew are considered as having performed their obligation, if they simply listen to its reading. Before the reading of the book of Esther, these blessings are recited:

"Blessed be the Lord, our God, King of the Universe, Who has sanctified us by His commandments, and has commanded us to read the Megillah."

"Blessed be the Lord, our God, King of the Universe, Who has wrought miracles for our fathers in days of old."

On the eve of Purim every worshipper puts his contribution toward charity into a plate or basket placed into the synagogue for collection.   The money thus procured is in some communities given to the precentor as a remuneration for his reading.   Both Chanukkah and Purim are in many synagogues made festivals for young people, and hence are celebrated by the presentation of plays dealing with the facts of the Chanukkah and Purim stories.

Such are in the main the ceremonial institutions, which we note during the public devotion in the synagogue on the different occasions of the year.

CHAPTER VI

Customs in the Home

The Jewish home is permeated by a
marked religious atmosphere. The injunction to speak when sitting in one's house of
the things God commanded has been put into
execution almost literally. From the time
the Jew takes possesson of a house he ex-
pects to make his residence, one ceremonial
institution after another is made to declare
the religion of the occupants. In compliance
with the Biblical passage, " Thou shalt write
them (the words of the law) upon the door
posts of thy house and upon thy gates," [1] we,
as a rule, find upon the upper part of the
right post of doors, leading into the residence
of a Jew, and of doors, leading into every
room of such residence, a small wooden,
glass, or metal tube varying from two to six
inches in length. This tube or case is known

[1] Deut. 6: 9.

by the name " Mezuzah," literally meaning " door post," and secondarily signifying object fixed to door post. It is always attached in a slanting position. The tube or case contains a small parchment scroll, made of the skin of a clean animal. The rules governing the writing of the paragraphs in the Mezuzah are the same as those to be observed in the writing of the scrolls and phylacteries. The passages contained in the Mezuzah are:

"Hear, O Israel, the Lord our God, the Lord is one.

And thou shalt love the Lord, thy God, with all thy heart, with all thy soul, and with all thy might.

And these words which I command thee, this day shall be in thy heart.

And thou shalt teach them diligently unto thy children, speaking of them when thou sittest in thy house, when thou walkest by the way, when thou liest down, and when thou risest up.

And thou shalt bind them for a sign upon thy hand and they shall be as frontlets between thine eyes.

And thou shalt write them upon the posts of the house and upon thy gates." [2]

The second section reads:

[2] Deut. 6: 4-9.

1 Mezuzoth   2 Mezuzah Scroll

" And it shall come to pass if ye shall hearken diligently unto my commandments, which I command you this day, to love the Lord, your God, and to serve him with all your heart, and with all your soul,

That I will give you the rain of your land in its due season, the first rain and the latter rain, that thou mayest gather in thy corn and thy wine and thine oil.

And I will send grass in thy fields for thy cattle, that thou mayest eat and be satisfied.

Take heed that your heart be not deceived and ye turn aside and serve other gods, and worship them:

And then the Lord's wrath be kindled against you and he shut up the heaven, that there be no rain and that the land yield not her fruit, and lest ye perish quickly from off the good land which the Lord giveth you.

Therefore shall ye lay up these, my words, in your heart, and in your soul, and bind them for a sign upon your hand that they may be as frontlets between your eyes.

And ye shall teach them to your children, speaking of them when thou sittest in thy house, when thou walkest by the way, when thou liest down and when thou risest up.

And thou shalt write them upon the door posts of thine house and upon thy gates." [3]

After the parchment has been finished, it is rolled up and put into the tube or case, which has a small opening, revealing the word שדי " Almighty," written on the back of the parchment.

[3] Deut. 11 : 13-20.

The Mezuzah must be examined periodically in order to ascertain whether it is in good condition. If the ink has faded the Mezuzah should be replaced by another. When the Mezuzah is attached to the door post a benediction is recited, praising God for having enjoined the law with reference to this institution.

A number of Jews, upon passing through a gate-way adorned with a Mezuzah, are in the habit of touching the Mezuzah with the hand and then kissing the hand, as a mark of respect. In the east there are Jewish homes which have Mezuzoth containing the whole decalogue. A similar custom obtains among Mohammedans who inscribe their doors and windows with passages from the Koran.

The object of the Mezuzah is to remind Jews of the need of sanctifying the home by means of religious teachings, so as to keep the home unpolluted from all evil. The Mezuzah is undoubtedly an amulet and forcibly recalls the protecting charm possessed by

the door posts of the ancient Israelites in
Egypt, as we read:

> "And ye shall take a bunch of hyssop and dip it in
> the blood that is in the basin and strike the lintel and
> the two side posts with the blood that is in the basin,
> and none of you shall go out at the door of his house
> until morning, for the Lord will pass through to
> smite the Egyptians; and when He seeth the blood
> upon the lintel and on the two side posts, the Lord
> will pass over the door and will not suffer the
> destroyer to come in unto your houses to smite
> you." [4]

The claim that the Mezuzah is an amulet,
protecting the occupants of the home against
harm from evil spirits, is justified by the be-
lief in the power of amulets among Jews, a
great number of whom are known to wear
them on their persons. The amulet,
"Kamea," used among Jews and worn by
them on their persons for purposes of protection against all sorts of misfortune, more
especially sickness, varies in design. A popular form is a piece of parchment with a
Hebrew inscription. Another form is an
ornament in the shape of a heart made of

[4] Ex. 12: 22-23.

some metal with " Shaddai," Almighty, inscribed on one side and the shield of David
engraved on the reverse side. In the collection of objects of Jewish ceremonial in the
National Museum at Washington there are,
in addition to the amulets of the character
already given, a medallion, a silver medal, a
silver coin, and two silver rings, used for
this purpose. The importance attached to
amulets may be recognized by the permission
the Shulchan Aruch grants to wear them on
the Sabbath,[5] whereas it forbids the carrying
of other portable things on the Sabbath, on
account of the fact, that carrying is considered a certain form of labor. Israel Abrahams tells, that betrothal rings inscribed with
the words " Mazal Tob," good luck, during
the middle ages were supposed to protect the
bride against the proverbial " evil eye," while
in more recent times seal rings were engraved
for a similar purpose with the name of God.[6]

[5] Orach Chayim 301.
[6] Jewish Life in the Middle Ages, p. 182.

In this connection it may be stated that
Abraham Ibn Ezra denounced amulets, together with other superstitions.

Though different in purpose from the
Mezuzah, an object found in most Jewish
homes should be mentioned in this connection. I refer to the so-called " Mizrach." It
is made either of paper, cardboard, silk or
velvet, and handsomely embroidered. Some
households own " Mizrachs " which are mas-
terpieces of art. The Mizrach gets its name,
which means East, from the object it serves.
When framed, it is usually suspended on the
eastern wall of the living room of the house,
in order to indicate the East, the direction, in
which occupants of the house turn when engaged in prayer. The verse usually found on
the top of the Mizrach is:

"From the rising of the sun unto its setting the
name of the Lord is praised." [1]

After the Jewish home is provided with
Mezuzoth and the family takes possession of
its home, the home is usually dedicated form-

[1] Ps. 113: 3.

ally by a religious ceremony, consisting of
the recitation of passages from the Biblical
and Talmudical writings.   The Biblical portions selected for this occasion are Psalms
30; 15; 101; 121; 127; 128; and 119, verses
9-16, 153-160, 81-88, 33-40 in the order here
given.   For the purpose of dedication some
one learned in the law is usually procured.

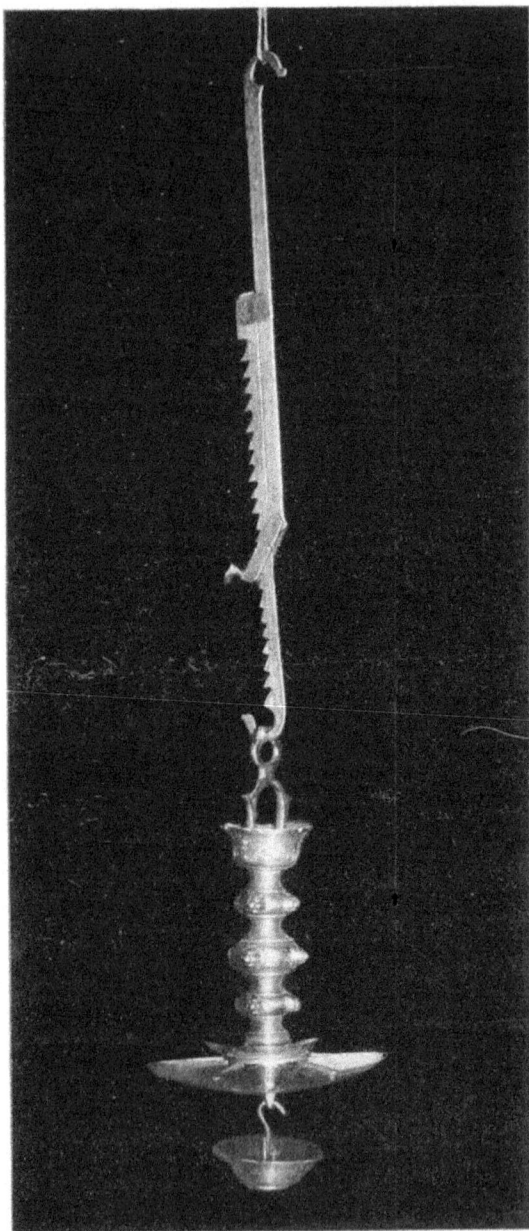

Sabbath Lamp

CHAPTER VII

Sabbath in the Home

Although attendance at synagogue is expected from Jews, on the ground that it has a tendency to strengthen the Jewish consciousness and solidarity, there are occasions when the home is made the scene of divine services. These occasions are the mornings and evenings of the week of mourning, " Shibah," following the death of some near relative (during which time the mourner is expected to abstain from the pursuit of his vocation) ; the anniversaries of the death of a relative; and wedding ceremonies (institutions, the details of which will be explained in subsequent chapters).

As in the discussion of the ceremonial institutions in vogue in the synagogue proper, we followed the holy seasons in their chronological order, so we shall follow them in chronological order in describing the institutions practiced in the home.

Before proceeding to them we shall take up the Sabbath.

The Sabbath among Jews is a day of joy, and the ceremonial institutions which mark it are therefore all expressive of its joyous character. While the head of the family is at the synagogue, welcoming in the public devotion the day of rest, the wife and mother, or in the case of her absence, the oldest female member of the home, decks the table in the dining room with a white cloth and places upon it two candlesticks, each of which contains a wax or tallow taper, kindled by her just before sundown, while reciting the benediction:

" Blessed be the Lord, our God, King of the Universe, Who has commanded us to kindle the Sabbath lights."

On the eve of festivals, when the same ceremony is observed, the word " festival " is substituted for the word " Sabbath " in the benediction.

The candlesticks are either of burnished brass or silver. In some instances a can-

Candlesticks and Candelabra

delabrum is used in place of the candlesticks, and in a number of cases homes are provided with Sabbath lamps, supplied with seven brackets for lights, and suspended from the ceiling of the living room.

In addition to the Sabbath lights, two loaves of bread, called " Berches " because symbols of God's blessing, the double portion of manna with which ancient Israel was provided on Friday,[1] are placed on the table directly in front of the seat to be occupied by the head of the family during the evening meal.   These " Berches " are usually baked at the home by the housewife, who is in duty bound to take the " Challah " (corresponding to the first part of the dough to be given to the priest),[2] which she places into the stove to be burnt.   This act is also accompanied by a benediction, in which God is blessed for commanding the separation of the Challah.

When the husband and father returns from the synagogue his children gather about

[1] Ex. 16: 22.
[2] Numb. 15: 17-21.

him, according to age, and he, placing his
hands upon their heads, invokes upon them a
benediction.   In the case of boys he pro-
nounces the words, " May God make thee
like Ephraim and Manasseh," and in the case
of the girls, " May God make thee like Sarah,
Rebeccah, Rachel and Leah," concluding in
both cases with the three-fold priestly benediction, " The Lord bless thee and preserve
thee, the Lord make his countenance to shine
upon thee, and be gracious unto thee; the
Lord lift up His countenance toward thee
and give thee peace."

Then follows the recitation of the Prov-
erbs 31 : 10-31, by the father, in which the
qualities of the virtuous woman are extolled,
in honor of the female head of the house.
Washing his hands (a custom enjoined before every service, especially before the meal
about to be served, because the table corresponds to the altar which demands the purity
of the priest), the husband proceeds to the
sanctification of the Sabbath, the Kiddush,
in the manner in which this ceremony took

place in the synagogue and as described in a
previous chapter.   When the blessing has
been recited over the wine, the goblet is
passed to every member of the family, according to age, each one of whom takes a
sip.   Then follows the benediction over the
loaves of bread, which reads:

" Blessed be the Lord, our God, King of the
Universe, Who brings bread out of the earth."

One of the loaves is cut and each person
at the table receives a small piece called the
" Motzie," i. e., a part of the loaf over which
a blessing has been pronounced. After sup-
per follow the grace after meals, and hymns
of praise which are known as " Zemiroth "
(psalms).

The lights in many Jewish homes are ex-
tinguished and the fires raked by a non-Jew,
engaged for this purpose, as by the Rabbinical interpretation of a Scriptural passage
Jews are forbidden to touch fire in any form.[3]

The same ceremony of breaking bread and
blessing the wine is observed on the eve of

[3] Ex. 35: 3.

holidays with some slight modification always suggested by the peculiar character of
the day celebrated. At the noon meal of the
Sabbath and holidays the blessing is recited
only over loaves of bread. The loaves, until
cut, are always covered by an embroidered
cloth reserved for this purpose. The noon
meal is also followed by songs of praise, as
is the meal on the eve of the previous day.
The " Habdalah " (distinction), celebrated
in the home at the close of the Sabbath, differs somewhat from its observance in the
public devotion of the synagogue. The male
members of the family drink the wine, while
all members of the family inhale the fragrance of the spices. In place of wine, if wine
cannot be procured, beer or milk may be
used. If there is no male head to the family,
mothers sanctify with Kiddush and close
with Habdalah the Sabbath in the home.

CHAPTER VIII

The Festivals in the Home

The holiday marked by elaborate ceremonial institutions in the home is Passover. Preparations are made for putting the home into holiday attire long before the arrival of the feast. For weeks sometimes housewives are busy removing the leaven out of the various apartments of their dwellings. When the house has been thoroughly cleansed the head of the family will, on the eve of the day preceding Passover, make a search in his house for leaven, gathering up everything of this kind and blessing God for having enjoined this custom as a religious duty. He then states, that all the leaven which has escaped his notice shall not be accounted as such but at the dust of the earth. About ten o'clock on the following day all the leaven gathered is burnt. During the afternoon the table is set for the Seder, " order," " service," which takes place upon the return of the male members of the family from the synagogue. The Seder is held in memory of Israel's exode from Egypt. The table is set as follows:

At the place immediately in front of the seat of him, who is to conduct the service, a dish is placed, on which are put three unleavened cakes (Matzoth), each one of which is covered separately. On the top of them are put a roasted egg, a roasted shank bone, the " Charoseth " (a mixture of scraped apples and almonds), " Maror " (bitter herbs, parsley and salt water). That which is wanted first is placed nearest to the leader of the service. Every one of these articles is emblematic of some special historical idea. The bitter herbs, usually consisting of horseradish, stand, on account of their pungent taste, for the hard work of the Israelites in Egypt. The Charoseth, on account of its brown color, is representative of the clay, out of which Israelites made bricks. The shank bone is the memorial of the paschal lamb. And the use of the egg, only a couple of centuries old and borrowed from Christians, is symbolical of the sacrifice brought on **each** day of the festival in the Temple.

During the service every participant drinks four cups of wine especially prepared for Passover. These four cups correspond to the four expressions of redemption used in the Bible, in connection with the story of Israel's liberation. The four expressions are הוצאתי " I have brought forth," גאלתי " I have redeemed," הצלתי " I have delivered," לקחתי " I have taken." [1]

In the great majority of families, the wine for this occasion is made of raisins. During the reading of the service the participants are to recline, expressive of the comparative freedom and ease Jews have enjoyed since their ancestors' slavery. The Passover is a family reunion and often brings together members of the same family living great distances apart. The dish containing the necessary articles is usually one designed for the Seder purpose. It is made either of earthenware or metal, and richly decorated.

[1] Ex. 6: 6-7.

The cups of wine are of silver, provided the means of the family will allow the purchase of such. It should be stated here that these utensils, as well as all others used during the Passover week, are never used at any other time of the year. When Passover has passed, the utensils are carefully stored away to keep them from all contact with either anything leaven or with the dishes used for leavened food.

The Seder service proceeds in the following order: First comes the sanctification of the day by Kiddush; then the washing of the hands; the eating of the parsley; the breaking of the middle cake in the dish (a part of which is called "Afikomen," by some distributed among the family after the meal, by others kept until the following year and burnt with the leaven on the eve of the subsequent Passover). Here follows an invitation to all who are needy to come and participate in the service. Then are told the stories of Israel's slavery, its exode from Egypt, and its development as a nation. Interspersed with

Kiddush Cup (Silver)   Passover Kiddush Goblet (Silver)

these narratives are comments by the Rabbis of the early Christian centuries and songs of praise to God. Then follow in the order here given the eating of the bitter herb, the serving of the evening meal, grace, psalms, songs, and special prayers.

The next festival observed in the home by special ceremonial is New Year. The ceremonial customary then is nothing more than the exchange of the compliments of the season. On this occasion relatives and friends visit one another and meet with the greeting, " Shanah Tobah," a Happy New Year, to which the person addressed responds, נם אתח or נם את lit. " also you," meaning " the same to you." If people find it impossible to see one another in person on this day, they exchange cards, expressing their good wishes with the inscription: לשנה טובה תכתב " May you be inscribed for a good year," with the phrase, " in the book of life " understood. These cards differ both in design and elaborateness. In some communities it is customary to eat honey with bread on the eve of the New Year, expressive of the wish that, as the bread is sweet, so may the experiences during the year to come be only the most pleasant.

A feast observed in the home by an interesting institution is the Feast of Tabernacles, celebrated, as has been stated in one of the preceding chapters, in commemoration of the fact, that the Israelites dwelt in booths, while wandering through the wilderness. Because Leviticus 23 : 43 commands, " In booths shall ye dwell," booths are erected for this festival in either the yard or on the roofs of Jewish homes. The booth has three sides of wood, while the fourth side or entrance is covered by a curtain. The roof consists of leaves and branches, closely put together, so that the sun may not annoy the family dining and sitting in the booth during the entire week of the festival. Everything which does not grow on the earth is unfit as material for the roof. The sides are usually hung with beautiful draperies, while the roof is hung with different kinds of fruit. The draperies are often

old curtains of the ark of the synagogue.
The work of construction begins immediately after the Day of Atonement.   The
height of the booth dare not exceed twenty
cubits, the measurement fixed by Rabbinical
law.   Nor is a booth allowed to be narrower
than the given size of four cubits.   Although
it is a duty to spend one's time in the booth
during this holiday, some people going even
so far as to sleep in it, the sick are exempt
from this obligation.   In case of rain, people
need not remain in the booth, although the
Kiddush (sanctification) and the Motzie
(breaking of bread), on the first night must
take place in it, despite inclement weather.

Chanukkah, the Feast of Dedication, observed in memory of the victories of Judas
Maccabeus over the Syrians, is celebrated in
the home, as in the synagogue, by the kindling of wax tapers or oil lamps by all male
members of the family.   In some instances
even the women and girls are permitted to
perform this religious duty.   The candelabra
used for this purpose are not always of costly

character. They are improvised at times out of wood or even egg shells. Because made a feast for children, owing to the youthfulness of the hero of the Chanukkah story, parents are in the habit of delighting the hearts of the little ones with presents of all kinds, as Christians are wont to do on Christmas. A favorite sport on this feast among Jews during the Middle Ages, mentioned by Israel Abrahams, was the propounding of arithmetical puzzles.[1] Card playing is on this feast not only permitted, but actually endorsed by Jewish tradition as a means of amusement. A well-known game of chance is that played with the Trendel (a top), made either of wood or metal. According to some the word " trendel " is a Judaized term from the German " Drähen," to turn, and according to others from " Trändel," to hesitate. Trendel, according to the latter derivation, would be the object, hesitating to decide upon what side to fall. The body of the top is a

[1] Jewish Life in the Middle Ages, p. 385.

Chanukah Lamp

cube, on each of the lateral sides of which is found a Hebrew letter. The four Hebrew letters are נ'ג'ה'ש the initials of the words constituting the sentence נס גדול היה שם " a great miracle happened there." In playing with the Trendel, each of the different persons engaged in the game puts a coin or nut into a common pot. The Trendel is spun, and the letter, which comes to view as the Trendel falls, indicates the gain or loss of the player. The letters are used as initials of German words. נ stands for " N," of " Nichts," and indicates that the player takes nothing out of the pot. The ג stands for " G," of " Ganz," and indicates that the whole pot belongs to the player. ה stands for " H," of " Halb," and indicates that the player gets half of the pot. ש stands for " St," of " Stellen," and indicates that the player must put a fixed fine into the pot. This game is not Jewish in origin. Nor do all Jews play it. It is confined to only German-speaking Jews. Stewart Culin of the

University of Pennsylvania, has treated it among other games played by different nations.

Purim is celebrated in the home by the interchange of presents between different families, known as " Shloach Manoth," the sending of gifts.[3] The poor especially are remembered with a goodly portion on this occasion. On the eve of the festival the table in many a home is set with sweets for visitors, more especially for masquers, who in every community go from home to home in large numbers and make carnival on this holiday. On Purim, too, card-playing is freely indulged in. These are in the main the institutions practiced in the Jewish home worthy of note.

The following chapters will lead us into a description of certain general religious customs and rites in vogue among Jews.

[3] Esther 9 : 22.

CHAPTER IX

Circumcision and Redemption of the First Born

In treating of the ceremonial institutions which are not confined either to the synagogue as such or to the Jewish home, let us discuss them in the order, in which the Jew encounters and experiences them in the course of his life.

The first institution claiming our attention is the hoary rite of circumcision. It consists, as the etymology of the English term implies, of the removal of the foreskin from the male organ by means of cutting. Its Hebrew equivalent is " Milah." There is no Jewish institution which has been preserved more faithfully and is violated less. In whatever particular a Jew may prove lax, he will rarely fail to perform the circumcision by means of the proper agent appointed for this purpose, if a son is born to him. The institution has met with general conformity, because of the

Biblical command at first enjoined upon
Abraham, and later upon the people of Israel.
It is Abraham concerning whom it is said:

"And God said unto Abraham, Thou shalt keep
my covenant, therefore, thou and thy seed after thee
in their generations.

This is my covenant which ye shall keep between
me and you, and thy seed after thee; every man
child among you shall be circumcised.

And ye shall circumcise the flesh of your foreskin; and it shall be a token of the covenant betwixt
me and you.

And he that is eight days old shall be circumcised
among you, every man child in your generations.
He that is born in the house, or bought with money
of any stranger which is not of thy seed.

He that is born in thy house and he that is bought
with thy money, must needs be circumcised; and my
covenant shall be in your flesh for an everlasting
covenant.

And the uncircumcised man child whose flesh of
his foreskin is not circumcised, that soul shall be cut
off from his people; he hath broken my covenant." [1]

The children of Israel are told:

"And in the eighth day the flesh of his (man
child's) foreskin shall be circumcised." [2]

Owing to the fact that circumcision was
the sign of God's adoption by Abraham, it

[1] Gen. 17: 9-14.
[2] Lev. 12: 3.

is known as ברית אברהם " The Abrahamitic covenant."

According to Jewish tradition, it is the duty of every father to circumcise his son. Should the father neglect his responsibility, the religious authorities look to its execution. And in the event that a male's circumcision is overlooked by those in authority in the congregation, said male, when grown, is obligated to provide for his own circumcision. One willing to remain uncircumcised is punished with the penalty of כרת " cutting off " from the congregation of God.

Originally every father was expected to circumcise his child, but in the course of time the office of professional operator, " Mohel," was created. At the present time the service is not infrequently delegated to a graduate physician, as circumcision is justly regarded a surgical operation.

The circumcision must take place on the eighth day after the child's birth and not earlier than sunrise. If a circumcision has for some cause or other been performed at night, blood, known as blood of the covenant, must be drawn by incision from the male organ of the child during the following day. In the case of weak children the circumcision is postponed until they are strong enough to undergo the operation. A sick child, for example, one suffering from fever, is not circumcised until seven days after its recovery. A child suffering from some local ailment, like sore eyes, is circumcised immediately after its recovery. The child born without foreskin has simply the drop of blood, constituting the blood of the covenant, taken from him by incision. The utmost precaution is always exercised not to endanger a child's life by circumcision. If the blood does not circulate properly in a child, or, if two children of the same family have died as a result of their circumcision, the circumcision must be postponed. If a child dies before the eighth day its circumcision should, according to the Shulchan Aruch, take place at the cemetery before burial, but without the recitation of the usual formula, although the dead child is given a name. The custom of circumcising dead children is not general.

Circumcision may take place even on Sabbaths. It may be performed in the home, or even in the synagogue. The synagogue is not often selected. The operation may be performed by means of any sharp instrument, either a lancet or scissors. A lancet is most generally employed.

The manner of the operation is as follows : The foreskin is stretched forward and held tight by some support, so that it does not slip back on the organ. It is then cut off close to the support and thrown into sand, because the promise was given to Abraham that his posterity would be as numerous as the grains of sand upon the seashore. Some wine is then sprinkled on the wound and on the face of the child in order to revive the child from weakness, consequent upon the loss of blood. The remaining skin of the organ is then cut, so that the head of the organ remains altogether exposed, an act termed " Periah," uncovering, without which the circumcision is null and void. Thereupon the operator takes some wine into his mouth and sucks the blood out of the wound, an act known as " Mezizah," and performed to prevent inflammation. Some healing powder is put on the wound, whereupon the organ is bandaged. The sucking of the blood has been abandoned in many communities, especially in such where practicing physicians perform the operation, and in its place antiseptics are used, as children have been known to become inoculated with the germs of disease by the traditional procedure.

The night preceding the circumcision is often spent by those, who expect to attend the acceptance of the boy into the Abrahamitic covenant, in the recitation of Psalms and Talmudical passages at the home of the child.

The most important person next to the operator at the circumcision is the " Sandek," God-father, or " Ba'al Berith," who holds the child while the circumcision is performed. The service accompanying the operation is the following :

As the child is brought into the room where the circumcision takes place, the company to witness the operation exclaims: "Blessed be he who comes in the name of God."

The father of the child then says:

"Behold I am prepared to perform the commandatory precept which the Creator, blessed be He, enjoined upon us, namely to circumcise my son, as it is written in the law. 'And at the age of 8 days every male throughout your generations should be circumcised.'"

The operator places the child, then, upon a chair symbolical of the throne of Elijah, Elijah being the angel of the covenant, according to the prophet Malachi, and says, "Behold I will send my messenger, and he shall prepare the way before me."[3]

The operator thereupon recites:

"This is the throne of Elijah—may he be remembered for good. For Thy salvation, O Lord, I have waited. For Thy salvation, O Lord, I have hoped. Thy commandments I have obeyed. For Thy salvation, O Lord, I have hoped. I rejoice because of Thy word, as one who finds abundant

---

[3] Mal. 3: 23.

booty. Unbounded peace comes to those, who cherish Thy law and obstacles never come into their path. Happy he, whom Thou choosest and whom Thou causest to approach, that he may dwell in Thy courts."

After this introduction the company responds:

"Let us be satisfied with the goodness of Thy house, Thy holy temple."

The God-father, who is seated upon a chair, now receives the child and holds it on his knees, while the operator says:

"Blessed be the Lord, our God, King of the Universe, Who has sanctified us with his commandments and enjoined upon us the circumcision."

Immediately after the circumcision the father intones:

"Blessed be the Lord, our God, King of the Universe, Who has sanctified us with his commandments, and commanded us to cause our sons to enter the covenant of our Father Abraham."

To this benediction the company responds:

"As he (the boy) has entered the covenant, so may he be permitted to enter the study of the law, the marriage state and the practice of good deeds."

Then the operator picks up a goblet of wine and says:

"Blessed be the Lord, our God, King of the Universe, Creator of the fruit of the vine.

Blessed be the Lord, our God, King of the Universe, Who from the womb sanctified the beloved (Isaac), who set a statute in his flesh and who sealed his off-spring with the sign of the holy covenant, therefore, with this reward. Oh, our living God, our Portion, our Rock, command the deliverance of the dearly beloved of our flesh from destruction for the sake of the covenant, Thou hast put on our flesh. Blessed be the Lord, Former of the covenant.

Our God, and God of our Fathers, preserve this child for his father and mother, and may he be called in Israel—(Here follows the Hebrew name of the child by which he is to be known.) Let the father rejoice over him that came from his loins, and let his mother be glad because of the fruit of her womb, as it is written in scriptures: 'let thy father and thy mother rejoice and let her that gave thee birth, be glad.' And as it is said: 'And I passed by thee, and saw thee weltering in thy blood, and said unto thee: In thy blood live.' And it is furthermore said: 'He hath remembered His covenant forever, the word which he commanded for a thousand generations; the covenant which He made with Abraham, and His oath unto Isaac, and which He confirmed unto Jacob for a statute, to Israel for an everlasting covenant.' And it is said: 'And Abraham circumcised his son, Isaac, when he was eight days old, as God had commanded him.'

Oh, give thanks unto the Lord, for He is good. His loving kindness endures forever. May this child (here the name is again mentioned), become great;

and as he has entered the covenant, so may he be permitted to enter the study of the law, the bond of marriage, and the practice of good deeds."

The God-father now drinks of the wine. A few drops are given to the infant. The goblet with the remainder is sent to the mother so that she may partake of its contents. The circumcision always concludes with a feast, followed by grace appropriate to the occasion and recited by the operator.[4]

While speaking of the circumcision of Jewish children, the adoption of non-Jews as proselytes may be taken into consideration. The Shulchan Aruch holds that non-Jewish males, seeking religious fellowship with Israel and the privileges resulting therefrom, must be subjected to circumcision. If the non-Jew has already been circumcised for hygienic reasons, the drop of blood, known as the blood of the covenant, referred to several times before, must be drawn from his genital organ by means of incision. If, for some reason or other, like weakness or

[4] For rules governing the circumcision, vide Shulchan Aruch, Yoreh Deah, 260, etc.

disease, the proselyte cannot be circumcised without dangerous consequences, he may be accepted by simply conforming to the two other conditions of admission, bathing and immersion. Attention should be called to the fact that at a meeting of American Reform Rabbis held in New York in 1892, the circumcision of proselytes was abolished as a condition of their admission into the Jewish faith.[5]

In this connection it may not be out of place to say a word on the attitude of Jews toward proselytes. It should be stated at the outset that Judaism is not a proselytizing faith. Non-Jews are accepted only if they apply for Jewish fellowship of their own free will and accord. Every conversion presupposes not only instruction in the principles and ceremonial institutions of Judaism but also the dissuasion of the prospective convert from his step. He must be made acquainted with the sad lot of persecution

[5] Vide "Year Book Central Conference of American Rabbis," 1892-1893.

which Israel has endured, and, only after the promise of willingness to share that lot with his newly adopted brethren can the convert hope to be accepted. In addition the pledge is exacted, that all children, born to the convert after entrance into the marriage state with a born Jew or Jewess, will be permitted to conform to the demands of the Abra-hamitic covenant.[*]

Since girls have no physical operation per-formed the question naturally arises, when do they receive their names? It is customary for the father and mother of the female child to go to the synagogue about six weeks after the girl's birth. This visit is usually made on the Sabbath. The father is called to the bema to be one of the eight persons to recite the usual benedictions over a sub-section of the weekly portion read from the scrolls. In the course of special blessings, which the father asks the precentor to make, he dele-gates the precentor to dedicate one to his new-born daughter and to give to her the

[*] Shulchan Aruch, Yoreh Deah, 268-270.

name by which she is to be known ever after,
and to dedicate another blessing to his wife.

The attitude of the synagogue toward female converts to Judaism is one of dissuasion, like its attitude toward males.

Another ceremony, to which male infants
are subjected, is that known as the " Redemption," פדיון הבן if the male child happens
to be the first born among the children of the
family.   The first born is always the first
born of the mother.   If a man marries a
widow with children and a boy is the first
fruit of the marriage, no Redemption is
necessary.   If the father is absent or sick at
the time of a son's Redemption, the Redemption must be observed by the mother.   This
institution takes place on the thirty-first day
after the child's birth.   If the day for the
Redemption happens to be a Sabbath or holiday, the ceremony is deferred until the next
following day, because, being a transaction
by means of coin, it would be a desecration
of the Sabbath.   The institution has its origin
in the fact that in the tenth plague, which

befell Egypt, and, in which the first born of
every Egyptian home was killed, the first
born of Israel was spared. The law is therefore laid down:

"Every firstling of an ass, thou shalt redeem with
a lamb, and if thou wilt not redeem it, then thou
shalt break his neck; and all the first born of man
among thy children shalt thou redeem." [7]

In Numbers both the age and the cost of
redemption are stipulated in the words:

"And those that are to be redeemed from a month
old shalt thou redeem according to thine estimation,
for the money of five sheckels, after the sheckel of
the sanctuary, which is twenty gerah." [8]

For the redemption of the child the parent
must go to one who is descended from the
priestly family of Aaron. The reason that
one of the descendants of Aaron officiates at
this ceremony is, because in the early days of
Israel the house of Aaron was selected in
place of the first born of Israel to minister in
the sanctuary. If the father of the child
happens to be of the family of Aaron or of
one of the less aristocratic Levitical clans, or,

[7] Ex. 13: 13.
[8] Numb. 18: 16.

if the mother is the daughter of an Aaronite or Levite, the child need not be redeemed. The amount of redemption money to be given to the priestly descendant is always the equivalent of five sheckels. This is about $2.50 in our currency. The money may be given in the form of a substitute if more agreeable or convenient. Should the father or mother neglect the ceremony of redemption, the child, when old, must of his own accord subject himself to it.

The service proceeds as follows: The father presents his child to the priest or Aaronite, and says:

"This my first born, is the first born of his mother; and the Holy One, Blessed be He, has commanded to redeem him as it is said: 'And those that are to be redeemed of them from a month old, shalt thou redeem, according to thine estimation, for the money of five sheckels, after the sheckels of the sanctuary, the sheckel being twenty gerahs.' And it is furthermore said: Sanctify unto me all the first born, whatsoever openeth the womb among the children of Israel, both of man and of beast; it is mine."

The father, then handing to the Aaronite the equivalent of five sheckels, is asked by him:

"What do you prefer? To give me thy first born son, the first born of his mother, or to redeem him for five selahs, which thou art by law obliged to give?"

The father answers:

"I prefer to redeem my son. Here is the value of his redemption, which I am by law obliged to give."

After the redemption money has been accepted and the child has been returned to the father, the father says:

"Blessed be the Lord, our God, King of the Universe, Who has sanctified us by his commandments and enjoined upon us the redemption of the son.

"Blessed be the Lord, our God, King of the Universe, Who has kept us alive, preserved us and permitted us to reach this season."

Holding the redemption money over the head of the child, the Aaronite declares:

"This is instead of that. This is in exchange of that. This is in remission of that. May it be the will of God, that as this child has entered the period of redemption, the child may be spared to enter the study of the law, the marriage state, and the practice of good deeds. Amen."

The Aaronite then places his hand upon the head of the child and says:

" May God make thee like Ephraim and Manasseh.
May the Lord bless thee and preserve thee.   May the
Lord let His countenance shine upon thee and be gracious unto thee.   May the Lord lift up His countenance toward thee and give thee peace.   The Lord
is thy keeper. The Lord is thy shade upon thy right
hand.   For length of days and years of life, and
peace they shall add to thee.   The Lord shall guard
thee against all evil.   He will guard thy life.

Amen."

After the redemption there is a feast similar to the one following the circumcision.

Here end the ceremonials of infancy.
Those remaining to be treated are the ceremonials of adolescence, manhood and of certain special occasions arising in the course of
life.

CHAPTER X

Bar Mitzvah

The thirteenth birthday of the Jewish boy
is one of the most important events of his
life. He is then considered as having attained his religious majority. The event is
usually celebrated by him both in the synagogue and home. Before, however, this is
done, he is obliged to make elaborate educational preparation. Long before the advent
of the important day, he is sent by his father
to a teacher, who instructs him in the whole
section or in one of the sub-sections of the
weekly Pentateuchal portion read on the Sabbath following his thirteenth birthday, according to the Jewish calendar, in order to
enable him to read the unpointed text from
the scrolls during the services. In addition
to the Pentateuchal section he is also
taught the accompanying prophetical portion.
While in some communities boys are permit-

ted to read the several parts of the Scriptures without the traditional melody, in the great majority of communities the reading with the melody (trope, or neginah) is not only expected, but actually demanded. During this period of instruction, the boy is further-more taught how to lay the phylacteries, which becomes a daily duty to be performed by him already three months before the thirteenth anniversary of his birth. When the day in question arrives, he is regarded a " Bar Mitzvah," a son of the commandment, by which is understood, a Jew expected to perform the precepts of the religion and punishable for their violation. According to tradition, the father, who is in duty bound to provide for the proper training of his son, is responsible for the son's every failure to comply in childhood with the laws of God. When, therefore, the son becomes a " Bar Mitzvah " the father thanks God for having freed him from further responsibility for laws transgressed by his son. The father then recites the benediction : " Praised be He (that is, God) Who has freed me from being responsible for this young man's conduct."

ברוך שפטרני מעונשו של זה

When the boy comes to the synagogue on the Sabbath of his Bar Mitzvah, he is called to the bema, where he sings the several sub-sections for others, who recite the traditional benedictions, usually saying the benedictions himself over the last and eighth sub-section, called, as will be remembered, " Maftir," the concluding portion.   Then the boy follows with the prophetical portion.   In some in-stances boys deliver addresses in the hearing of the assembled worshippers, in which are set forth the duties and benefits of the Jew. Upon returning from the public devotion, the mid-day meal is made a family feast, and, during the course of the same, the " Bar Mitzvah " delivers a speech, in which he thanks his parents and relatives for the love and care enjoyed at their hands.   On this occasion the boy is as a rule the recipient of gifts from relatives and friends.

The reason assigned for the age at which
a boy becomes a " Bar Mitzvah " is a statement made in the Mishnah to this effect:

"At five one must begin the study of the Bible,
at ten that of the Mishnah, and at thirteen one
must assume the commandments, etc." [1]

Whether this is the real reason for the
foundation of the institution is questionable.
We are inclined to believe that thirteen was
fixed as the age of the Jew's religious majority because in the East boys attain their
physical maturity at about this age.   As a
religious institution to be celebrated according to the manner described, it is no doubt the
result of Christian influences [2] and corresponds to the rite of Confirmation in the
Church.   Its existence in the synagogue cannot be traced further back than the fourteenth century. [3]

Girls are not subjected to this ceremony,
as they cannot be expected to perform re-

[1] Aboth 5: 24.
[2] Dembitz, "Services in Synagogue and Home"
p. 263.
[3] Jewish Life in the Middle Ages, p. 32; Loew,
"Lebensalter" p. 210.

ligious obligations, which have to be executed at a definite time (a point dwelt upon
in a previous chapter).

The Bar Mitzvah ceremony, in the elaborateness given to it in previous centuries, has
fallen into disuse in many communities.
With the ever-lessening attention paid by
Jews to the study of Hebrew, a boy, who becomes a Bar Mitzvah, frequently does no
more than recite the benedictions over a sub-
section of the law read to him by the precentor of the synagogue. In those communities
where the Bar Mitzvah ceremony has either
disappeared altogether or been modified as
stated, an institution known as Confirmation, to which both boys and girls are admitted, has taken the place of the Bar Mitzvah.
It may be celebrated at any time. In America
" Shebuoth," Feast of Weeks, is generally
selected, because of the existing tradition,
that on the sixth day of Sivan, the third
month, the law was given to Israel at Mt.
Sinai. This time is, therefore, best suited to
impress on Confirmants their religious

responsibility.   The age of Confirmation is about the same as that of the Bar Mitzvah, although an effort is now being made to raise the age of Confirmation, on account of the need of a more pronounced mental maturity for the proper comprehension of the subjects taught classes prepared for this ceremony. Confirmation was first introduced into the synagogue at Cassel, Westphalia, in 1810.

CHAPTER XI

Marriage

The ceremony following that of Bar Mitzvah or Confirmation, in the life of the Jew, is that of marriage. The age of marriage differs greatly. In some sections Jews marry earlier than in others. The practice is regulated for the most part by the custom in vogue among non-Jews. Israel Abrahams tells, that " the early age at which marriages occur must have been partly responsible for the chastity of the Jews in the middle ages." [1] Since the Mishnah fixes the eighteenth year of one's life as the age of marriage,[2] a man unmarried after this time is, in many communities, regarded as not having conformed with inviolable tradition. The Shulchan Aruch states: " Every Jewish man should marry at eighteen, and he who marries earlier

[1] Jewish Life in the Middle Ages, p. 90.
[2] Aboth 5: 24.

is more meritorious. No one, however, should marry earlier than thirteen years of age." [3]

In the selection of a spouse Jews and Jewesses must be cautious not to choose any one with whom wedlock is forbidden on account of consanguinity, affinity, chastity, or on religious grounds. The marriages forbidden on account of consanguinity and affinity are those stipulated in or based upon Leviticus 18: 11-21, and there regarded as incest. Marriages forbidden on account of chastity are, for example, the marriage with one's divorced wife, after she had been married to another man; the marriage of adulterers; the marriage between a divorced woman and a witness in her divorce case; and the marriage of a legitimate child of one family with an illegitimate child of another. Marriages forbidden on religious grounds are, for example, the marriage of Jews with non-Jews; the marriage of the childless widow of a man, who leaves an unmarried

[3] Eben Haezer 1: 3.

brother, with a stranger; and the marriage of an Aaronite with a divorced woman. For further particulars as to restrictions placed on the Aaronite in matters of marriage we refer to the 21st chapter of Leviticus.[4]

A marriage can take place any day of the week excepting on a Sabbath or a holiday. Every Jewish marriage presupposes three conditions—the consent of both parties to the marriage, their mental soundness, and their legal age.

In some communities the professional match-maker, " Shadchan," plays a prominent part in the arrangement of marriages between young people. When he finds two persons, who in his opinion are fitted as partners for one another, he takes the initiative in bringing them together. The Shadchan is undoubtedly a remnant of the Crusades, during which, owing to the disintegration of society through massacre and expulsion, Jewish men and women had to be brought together by an agent of the Shadchan's kind.[5]

[4] Lev. 21: 6, 7, 14.
[5] Jewish Life in the Middle Ages, p. 170.

The marriage ceremony consists of two parts—the betrothal, " Erusin," and the nuptials, " Nissuin," which before the sixteenth century were performed separately. The betrothal often precedes the nuptials by from one month to a whole year. The ceremony is performed by a Rabbi, although during the Middle Ages either the groom himself or some guest at the wedding pronounced the customary benedictions. While the omission of the benedictions referred to would not invalidate a marriage, the benedictions glorifying God, are, as a rule, nevertheless recited, since according to Jewish law marriage is a divine institution. A Jewish marriage is conducted as follows:

The bride and groom, who are expected to fast on the day of their marriage, as a mark of their penitence for wrongs committed in the early part of their life, proceed to the altar. The bride is led by her father and the groom by his mother. They then take their places under a nuptial canopy, " Chuppah." The Chuppah, which is made either of silk or

satin, and is often handsomely embroidered
with the words קול חתן " the voice of the
groom," קול כלה " the voice of the bride,"
קול ששון " the sound of joy," and קול שמחה
" the sound of gladness," is supported by
four staves, one on each corner, and held by
four guests. Instead of an embroidered
covering in silk or satin, a large praying
scarf, " Talith," is often used.

The person consummating the marriage
opens with the words:

" Blessed be he who comes in the name of the
Lord. We bless you out of the house of the Lord.
Come, let us worship and bow down. Let us kneel
before the Lord our Maker.
Serve the Lord with Joy. Come before Him, with
shouting."

Thereupon Psalm 100 is intoned, followed
by these words:

" May He, Who is Mighty, Blessed and Great,
above all things bless the bridegroom and the bride."

After this introduction the officiating
clergyman is wont to give a charge, upon the
conclusion of which blessings of betrothal

are intoned. Lifting up one of the two goblets of wine, the clergyman says:

"Blessed be the Lord, our God, King of the Universe, Who creates the fruit of the vine.

Blessed be the Lord, our God, King of the Universe, Who has sanctified us by His commandments and commanded us concerning forbidden marriages; Who denied those, that are betrothed, but sanctioned for us such as are wedded to us, by means of the canopy and the sacred covenant of wedlock. Blessed be the Lord, Who sanctifies his people, Israel, by means of the canopy and the sacred covenant of wedlock."

The bride and groom having drunk from the goblets of wine just blessed, the groom proceeds to place a ring upon the forefinger of the bride's right hand, saying:

"Behold, thou art consecrated unto me by means of this ring, according to the laws of Moses and Israel."

Here follows the reading of the marriage contract, "Kethubah," given to the bride. The seven nuptial blessings are then recited by the clergyman, who lifts up a second goblet of wine, saying:

"Blessed be the Lord, our God, King of the Universe, Who creates the fruit of the vine.

Blessed be the Lord, our God, King of the Universe, Who creates all things for His Glory.

Blessed be the Lord, our God, King of the Universe, Creator of man.

"Blessed be the Lord, our God, King of the Universe, Who made man in his image, according to His likeness, and prepared for him out of His own being, an everlasting fabric.

Blessed be the Lord, Creator of Man. May she who was barren, i. e., Zion, be exceedingly glad and exult when her children are gathered within her in joy.

Blessed be the Lord, Who makes Zion glad because of her children.

Cause the loved companions to rejoice, even as Thou didst in days of old gladden Thy creatures in the garden of Eden. Blessed be the Lord, Who causes the bridegroom and the bride to rejoice.

Blessed be the Lord, our God, King of the Universe, Who created joy and gladness, bridegroom and bride, mirth and exultation, pleasure and delight, love and brotherhood, peace and fellowship.

May there be heard soon in the cities of Judah and in the streets of Jerusalem the voice of joy and gladness, the voice of the bridegroom and the voice of the bride, the jubilant voice of the bridegrooms from their canopies and of youths from their feasts of song.

Blessed be the Lord, Who causes the bridegroom to rejoice with the bride."

The young couple then drink from the second goblet. A glass is broken by the bridegroom and the three-fold priestly blessing is intoned as a fitting conclusion of the ceremony.

The details of the ceremony have their symbolical significance. The Chuppah represents the home of the couple which is to be permeated by the religious spirit. The two goblets of wine represent the cups of joy and sorrow and the bridegroom's and bride's drinking from both is expressive of their willingness to share the joys and sorrows of life. The ring, which no doubt originated in medieval times, is a substitute for the coin, by means of which marriages were originally consummated. It must be made of pure gold and be devoid of gems. Its purity is symbolic of conjugal fidelity; and gems are omitted, as their exact value cannot be estimated. The breaking of a glass is for good luck. It is supposed to forestall all misfortune due to excessive rejoicing. The custom is no doubt based on a legend, which tells, that when Rabbina's son was married, Rabbina noticed that the guests were too hilarious. In order to check their glee he broke before them a

white porcelain vase worth two hundred
zuzim, equal to $100 in our currency.[*]

The Kethubah, or contract, which pro-
tected women against penury in the days
when women could be divorced against their
will, a condition changed by Rabbenu Gersham, a teacher of the eleventh century,
reads:

"On......(day of the week), the......
day of the month......in the year......
A. M., according to the Jewish reckoning,
here, in the city of......Mr.......son of
......said to the virgin......daughter of
......: Be thou my wife in accordance with
the laws of Moses and Israel, and I will work
for thee, honor, support and maintain thee,
in accordance with the custom of Jewish
husbands, who work for their wives, honor,
support and maintain them. I will furthermore set aside two hundred denarii to be thy
dowry, according to the law, and, besides,
provide thy food, clothing, and necessaries,

[*] Tosephoth Berachoth, 31, a.

and live with thee in conjugal relations
according to universal custom.

Miss......on her part consented to become his wife. The marriage portion which
she brought from her father's house in silver,
gold, valuables, clothes, etc., amounts to
...... Mr.......the bridegroom, consented to increase this amount from his
property with the sum of......making in
all...... He furthermore declared: I
take upon myself and my heirs the responsibility for the amount due according to this
contract and of the marriage-portion, and of
the additional sum (by which I promised to
increase it), so that all this shall be paid from
the best part of my property, real and per-
sonal, such as I now possess or may hereafter acquire. All my property, even the
mantle on my shoulders, shall be mortgaged
for the security of the claims above stated,
until paid now and forever. Thus, Mr.
......, the bridegroom, has taken upon
himself the fullest responsibility for all obligations of this Kethubah, as customary in

ב   בשבת
שנת חמשה אלפים ושש מאות וארבעים
לבריאת עולם למנין שאנו מנין כאן
איך ר"

אמר לה להדא בתולתא

הוי לי לאנתו כדת משה וישראל ואנא אפלח ואוקיר
ואיזון ואפרנס יתיכי ליכי כהלכות גוברין יהודאין דפלחין
ומוקרין וזנין ומפרנסין לנשיהון בקושטא ויהבנא ליכי מהר
בתוליכי כסף זוזי מאתן דחזו ליכי מדאורייתא ומזוניכי
וכסותיכי וסיפוקיכי ומיעל לותיכי כאורח כל ארעא
וצביאת מרת   בתולתא דא והות
ליה לאנתו ודין נדוניא דהנעלת ליה מבי
כין בכסף בין בזהב בין בתכשיטין במאני דלבושא
בשימושי דירה ובשמושא דערסא מאה זקוקים כסף
צרוף וצבי ר'   חתן דנן
והוסיף לה מן דיליה מאה זקוקים כסף צרוף אחרינ
כנגדן סך הכל מאתים זקוקים כסף צרוף וכך אמר
ר'   חתן דנן אחריות
שטר כתובתא דא נדוניא דן ותוספתא דא קבלית עלי
ועל ירתי בתראי להתפרע מכל שפר ארג נכסין וקנינין
דאית לי תחות כל שמיא דקנאי ודעתיד אנא למקני
נכסין דאית להון אחריות ודלית להון אחריות בלהון יהון
אחראין וערבאין לפרוע מנהון שטר כתובתא דא נדוניא
דן ותוספתא דא ואפילו מן גלימא דעל כתפאי בחיי
ובמותי מן יומא דנן ולעלם ואחריות וחומר שטר כתובתא
דא נדוניא דן ותוספתא דא קבל עליו ר'
הן דנן כחומר כל שטרי כתובות
ותוספתת דנהגין בבנת ישראל העשויין כתיקון חכמינו
זכרונם לברכה דלא כאסמכתא ודלא כטופסי דשטרי
וקנינא מן ר'
הן דנן למרת
בתולתא דא בכל מה דכתב
ומפורש לעיל במנא דכשר למקניא ביה הכל שריר וקים

regard to the daughters of Israel and in accordance with the strict ordinances of our
sages of blessed memory; so that this document is not to be regarded as an illusory
obligation, or as a mere form of documents.

In order to render the above declarations
and assurances of the said bridegroom to
the said bride perfectly valid and binding, we
have applied the legal formality of symbolical delivery."

To this document are usually attached the
signatures of the bridegroom and two witnesses and sometimes also the signature of
the officiating clergyman.[1]

The ceremony is often preceded by the
reading of the regular afternoon service,
" Minchah," and is itself never performed
among more conservative Jews without the
presence of the usual devotional quorum of
ten men. It is conducted either at the home
of the bride or at the synagogue. After the
ceremony a family feast is held, followed by

[1] Vide Mielziner, " Jewish Law of Marriage and
Divorce " for additional details.

a special prayer of grace. These are the main characteristics of the Jewish marriage. In many communities there are some special features peculiar to them and not known by others. Where such is the case, the special features may be traced to similar customs in vogue among local non-Jews.

CHAPTER XII

Although the Jew regards marriage a divine institution, and hence one to be maintained throughout the husband's and wife's life, he favors the discontinuance of the marriage state under certain well defined and reasonable conditions. The Jewish divorce laws are based on the following passages:

"When a man hath taken a wife and married her, and it come to pass, that she find no favor in his eyes, because he hath found some uncleanliness in her, then let him write her a bill of divorcement and give it in her hand, and send her out of his house. And when she is departed out of his house she may go and be another man's wife." [1]

According to the Biblical passages just cited, the right of divorcing was granted to the husband with no provision of the same right to the wife. In order to prevent the abuse of this privilege the " Kethubah," marriage contract, was introduced, which stipu-

[1] Deut. 24: 1-2.

lated a dowry for the wife, in case of her divorce; while, since the days of Rabbenu Gersham, a teacher of the eleventh century, restrictions in the right of divorce were imposed also on the husband. At the present time no divorce can take place according to Jewish law, except upon common agreement of husband and wife. Nor is the right to sue for divorce any longer confined to the husband. The wife enjoys the same privilege to free herself from an unhappy union. A wife, as well as a husband may sue for divorce on the ground of adultery, immorality or loathsome disease. In addition to these reasons a wife may sue for divorce on account of nonsupport or desertion. It must, however, be remembered, that while divorce is permitted, Jews, as a rule, seek to avoid a legal separation between husband and wife. The shame attaching to divorce may be recognized in the well-known Rabbinical sentiments, " He who divorces his wife is hated before the Lord "; " God's altar sheds tears for him who divorces the wife of his youth."

באחד בשבת   ימים לירח   שנת חמשת אלפים ישש מאות וחמשים

לבריאת עולם למנין שאנו מנין כאן בבאלטימארע דמתקריא באלטימאר

מתא דיתבא על נהר פאטאפסקא ועל כף ימא ועל מי מעינות אנא

העובד היום בבאלטימוארע דמתקריא באלטימוארע מתא דיתבא על נהר

פאטאפסקא ועל כף ימא ועל מי מעינות צביתי ברעית נפשי בדלא אניקא

ושבקית ופטרית ותרוכית יתיכי ליכי אנת אנתתי

העומדת היום בבאלטימוארע דמתקריא באלטימוארע מתא דיתבא על נהר פאטאפסקא

ועל כף ימא ועל מי מעינות דהוית אנתתי מן קדמת דנא וכדו פטרית

ושבקית ותרוכית יתיכי ליכי דיתהוייין רשאה ושלטאה בנפשיכי למהך להתנסבא לכל

גבר די תיצבייין ואניש לא ימחא בידיכי מן יומא דנן ולעלם והרי אתמותרת לכל אדם

ודן די יהוי ליכי מנאי ספר תרוכין ואגרת שבוקין וגט פטור ...

כ...ת בושה...ה ...וישר...אב

עדים

עדים

Bill of Divorce

The divorce is always conducted in the presence of the religious quorum of ten men, although originally it was conducted in the presence of two witnesses. It consists of the delivery of the bill of divorce, " Get," by the husband to the wife. The bill, written in a mixture of Hebrew and Aramaic, reads as follows:

" On the.....day of the week, the..... day......of the month......in the year ......of the creation of the world, according to the number we reckon here,......the city, which is situated on the river......and contains wells of water, I.....son of..... who stand this day in......the city situated on the river......and containing wells of water, do hereby consent, with my own will, without force, free and unrestrained, to grant a bill of divorce to thee, my wife..... daughter of......who hast been my wife from time past, and with this I free, release and divorce thee that thou mayest have control and power over thyself from now and hereafter, to be married to any man whom thou mayest choose and no man shall hinder thee from this day forevermore, and thus thou art free for every man.   And this shall be unto thee from me a bill of divorce, a letter of freedom, and a document of dismissal, according to the laws of Moses and Israel.''

The document is always signed by two witnesses.[2]

The laws, governing the writing of the bill of divorce, as found in the Shulchan Aruch,[3] are of interest.   We shall cite only a few of the more important.   The bill of divorce must be written in twelve lines, with durable ink, on parchment, prepared like that of the scrolls of the law.   It must not be mutilated.   It must be delivered to the wife in person, either by the husband or by an agent appointed for this purpose.   It must not be written on Friday.   It must be free from mistakes or repetitions.   Before it is written the writer must draw thirteen lines

[2] Mielziner, "Jewish Law of Marriage and Divorce," and Amram "Jewish Divorce Law."

[3] Eben Haezer, 120-153.

across the parchment, twelve for the bill
itself and a thirteenth line divided into two
halves for the signatures of the two witnesses. Every letter must stand by itself;
that is, it must not be connected with others.
Nor must the letters of one line run into
another line, either above or below. The
witnesses and writer, husband and wife, must
not be in any way related. The bill of divorce must be handed to the wife while it is
day and not at night.

An institution which is in vogue in many
communities, and reminds us of divorce pro-
ceedings, is " Chalitzah," the act of loosening. By means of it the childless widow of
a man is emancipated from the duty of
marrying the dead man's eldest single
brother. A marriage between a childless
widow and her husband's single brother is
called " Yibbum," from the Hebrew " Ya-
bam," brother-in-law. Its English equivalent
is " Levirate." This peculiar marriage,
called " Levirate marriage," together with

the form of emancipation from it, is based
on the following Biblical law :

"If brethren dwell together and one of them die
and have no child, the wife of the dead shall not
marry without unto a stranger; her husband's
brother shall go in unto her, and take her to him
to wife, and perform the duty of a husband's brother
unto her.

And it shall be that the first born which she bear-
eth shall succeed in the name of his brother, which
is dead, that his name be not put out of Israel.

And if the man like not to take his brother's wife,
then let his brother's wife go up to the gate unto the
elders and say: My husband's brother refuseth to
raise up unto his brother a name in Israel; he will
not perform the duty of my husband's brother.

Then the elders of his city shall call him and
speak unto him, and if he stand to it and say: ' I
like not to take her ';

Then shall his brother's wife come unto him, in
the presence of the elders, and loose his shoe from
off his foot and spit in his face, and shall answer
and say: ' So shall it be done unto that man that
will not build up his brother's house.'

And his name shall be called in Israel, the house
of him that hath his shoe loosed." *

The object of the " levirate " marriage
was not only, as shown in the Biblical text
quoted, to preserve the name of the dead
husband but also to keep the tribal portion

* Deut. 25 : 5-10.

of the dead husband in his tribe, as the
brother became, according to the old Israelitish Agrarian law the heir of the dead man's
property by marrying his wife.   The ceremony attending the separation of all ties between the widow and brother-in-law consists of the loosening of the brother-in-law's
shoe by the widow, whereupon she spits out
before him saying: " So shall it be done unto
the man, that will not build up his brother's
house."   Three judges, for the most part the
Rabbi, and chief officers of the congregation,
must attend the " Chalitzah."   These must
be related neither to one another nor to any
of the parties seeking the emancipation.
During the ceremony the religious quorum
of ten men is required.   The " Chalitzah "
dare not take place before ninety-two days
after the death of the husband.   The widow
is expected to fast on the day of her emancipation.   The shoe to be loosened is that on
the right foot of the brother-in-law.   During the entire ceremony, the judges are expected to sit and the parties to the separation

are obliged to stand. When the shoe is loosened the brother-in-law must stand firm upon the right foot and in no way assist the widow while she loosens the shoe with her right hand. She is not permitted to use the left hand. When the shoe is off, she throws it from her as far as possible. The widow then expectorates before the brother-in-law and all persons present exclaim three times: " The bare-footed." The brother-in-law returns the shoe to the Judges, from whom he originally received it, and they say to him: " May God be gracious unto thee, that the daughters in Israel will never have to marry the brother of a dead husband, or receive ' Chalitzah ' from him." At the " Chalitzah " a document is handed by the brother-in-law to the widow as a sign of cessation of all mutual obligations.[5]

In order to prevent brothers-in-law from abusing the " Chalitzah " by exacting large indemnity from the widows who often desire to be emancipated, brothers-in-law are

[5] Shulchan Aruch, Eben Haezer, 169.

obliged to sign a document " Shtar Chalitzah," on the day of a young couple's marriage, stipulating, that they will give " Chalitzah " without the claim of a remuneration.
In many communities this ceremony has disappeared entirely.   The conference of American Rabbis held in Philadelphia in 1869 and
the one held at Augsburg in 1871 ruled the
Chalitzah as unnecessary for Jews of the
present time.[6]

[6] Mielziner, " Jewish Law of Marriage and Divorce."

CHAPTER XIII

Mourning Customs

The last ceremonial in the life of a man is the death bed scene and the mourning which follows in his honor. It is these which we will consider now.

When the persons surrounding a patient notice that there is no hope for recovery and that death is a matter of only a very short time, they prevail upon the patient to make a confession of his guilt. For this purpose the Rabbi is not summoned. Any person may receive the confession, as the confession is not analogous to the last sacrament of the Church. The last words of the dying Jew are always: "Hear, O Israel, the Lord is our God, the Lord is one." If the patient is too weak to pronounce these words, those in attendance do so for him. In the case of a woman's death, those called in to be with the dying, are usually

women. As the patient closes his eyes all
present say: ברוך דין אמת " Praised be Thou,
O Judge of Truth! "

Among most Jews, when death takes
from them some near relative, a garment
is rent by each one as a sign of grief. This
rending is termed " Keriah." The moment
a person dies, a light is kindled, which is
kept burning for thirty days and is rekindled at every anniversary of the person's
death. Light, as has been said before, is the
thing with which the Bible compares the
soul of man. When the light is rekindled
on the occasion of an anniversary, it is kept
burning for twenty-four hours, from sundown to sundown. From the moment that
the earth covers the coffin, containing the
remains of the departed, the mourning of the
family begins. It is then that its members
commence to recite the " Kaddish," mourner's benediction, at every service during their
period of mourning. There are several forms
of the " Kaddish," the language of which is
Aramaic. The most common form is:

" The great name of God be exalted, and sanctified in the world, which He created, according to His will.

May His Kingdom be established in your life, and in your days, in the life of the whole house of Israel, now and forever. Amen.

His great name be glorified forever and aye.

Render praise and benediction, glory and exaltation. Speak of eminence and excellency. Sing songs and hymns to His hallowed name. Give praise to Him Who is exalted high above all benedictions and hymns which are uttered in the world. Amen.

May the Lord of Heaven and earth grant eternal peace and a full participation of the bliss of eternal life, and mercy to Israel, to all the righteous and to all who departed this life in the fear of the Lord. Amen.

May heaven's fullness of peace and life be granted unto us and all Israel. Amen.

May He, Who makes peace in His heavens high, also bestow peace upon us and all Israel. Amen." [1]

For seven days, known as " Shibah," including the Sabbath, on which there is no mourning, and the holidays which modify or set aside the mourning, the mourners, namely the members of the immediate family of the departed, sit either upon the floor or on low stools, as a sign of their abject condition and

[1] This English rendering is taken from Dr. Wise's Minhag America.

profound grief. During this period every
vocational duty is discontinued. On every
morning and evening of the " Shibah," services are conducted in the house of mourning.
Friends usually send mourners their food.
In some communities the period of this
mourning, perhaps appropriately termed
" first mourning," is shortened to three
days, and, in others to one day, owing to
the inability of many people to discontinue
business for seven days without incurring
great losses. On the Sabbath eve, after the
burial of a relative, the mourners, who remain in waiting in the ante-chamber of the
synagogue during the early part of the service, are escorted into the synagogue proper
by the precentor, just before he welcomes
the Sabbath. To do this the precentor
leaves the bema, and approaches the door
with words of consolation. The " Shibah " is followed by a second mourning,
" Shloshim," thirty days, of which the " Shibah " forms a part. For eleven months,
from the time of burial, mourners attend

every day all services in the synagogue, in
order to recite the " Kaddish." During the
first week, the mourner does not go to the
synagogue, as services are held in the house
of mourning. Eleven months were designated, undoubtedly in order to separate the
year of mourning from the immediately following year. According to the " Shulchan
Aruch " the length of time, during which the
" Kaddish " is recited, varies according to
the relationship of the surviving kinsman to
the departed. Modern usage, however, provides for its recitation for eleven months
for every bereavement in one's immediate
family.

Another occasion of hallowing the memory of the dead, as well as praising God for
one's bereavement, is the Memorial service
conducted periodically during the year in the
public service of the synagogue.

The customs of burial and mourning are
not the same in all countries. Attention
should be called to the fact that the Jewish
dead are seldom buried in anything but a

plain white linen shroud and in simplest coffin.

This uniformity of the attire of the corpse is based on the desire to conform to the Biblical passage: " Naked came I out of my mother's womb and naked shall I return thither," [2] not to mention the desire to emphasize in death the equality of all men.

[2] Job 1: 21.

CHAPTER XIV

RITUALISTIC SLAUGHTERING

Before closing the treatment of Jewish ceremonial institutions, a word should be said about the ritualistic slaughtering of animals fit for food among Jews. A few statements will suffice to convey a fairly definite idea concerning it. The method of killing animals for food among Jews consists of severing the trachea and œsophagus of the animal by means of a knife, entirely devoid of notches, so that the blood may flow easily out of the body through the slit made. Slaughtering is not directly commanded in the Pentateuch. The verse on which slaughtering is based is:

"Only be sure that thou eat not the blood for the blood is the life. And thou mayest not eat the blood with the life." [1]

The knives, " Challafim," used differ in size, according to the size of animals to be

[1] Deut. 12 : 23.

slaughtered. For fowl there is a small
knife, for small cattle a larger one, and for
big cattle one of extraordinary size. The
act of slaughtering is known as " Shechi-
tah " and the person performing the act
is titled " Shochet," a slaughterer. The
" Shochet " must be a person qualified by
knowledge. His examination before com-
petent Judges, if passed successfully is
called " Kabbalah." The " Shochet," after
a careful examination of its various vital
organs, passes upon the fitness of the animal
slaughtered for food. If he finds the animal
sound he seals the parts with the mark " Ko-
sher " meaning, " fit for food " in contra-
distinction to " Terefah " meaning " unfit,"
but originally signifying something torn by
a wild animal. In this connection the following passage is of interest. " And ye
shall be holy men unto me; neither shall ye
eat any flesh that is torn of beasts in the
field; ye shall cast it to the dogs." [2]   All

[2] Ex. 22: 31.

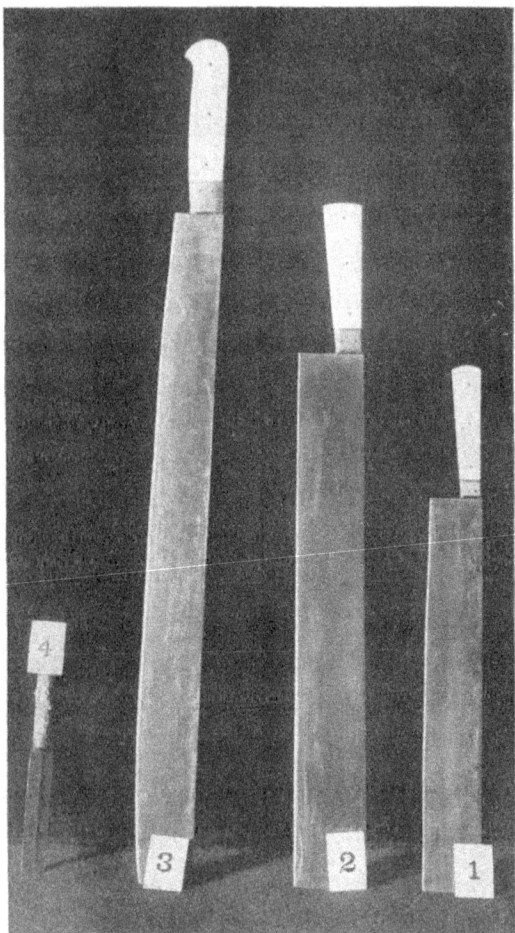

1 Knife for Slaughtering of Fowl
2 Knife for Slaughtering of Small Cattle
3 Knife for Slaughtering of Large Cattle
4 Circumcision Knife

animals are " Terefah " which are found un-
sound, have died,[3] or are killed by other
means than that of slaughtering.   It is
hardly necessary to state, which animals are
permitted for food among Jews.   Leviticus
11 and Deuteronomy 14 are explicit on this
subject.   Let this general principle suffice
as a statement of the guiding rule observed.
Of animals, living on the dry ground, only
such are eaten, which chew their cud and
divide their hoofs, while of animals, living
in the water, only such are eaten which
have scales and fins.   Attention should,
however, be called to this point, that certain
parts of animals, permitted for food, are
forbidden.   They are blood,[4] fat,[5] and the
hind quarter on account of containing the
sciatic nerve.   The hind quarter is avoided
as food on account of the narrative in Genesis, which concluding the story of Jacob's
wrestling with the angel of the Lord, tells :

---

[3] Deut. 14 : 21.
[4] Deut. 12 : 23.
[5] Lev. 7 : 23.

"Therefore the children of Israel, eat not of the sinew which shrank, which is upon the hollow of the thigh unto this day, because he touched the hollow of Jacob's thigh in the sinew that shrank."[6]

Another fact to be mentioned here is, that nothing made of milk in any form, like butter or cheese, is used by Jews together with meat or fat of any kind, the meat of fish alone being exempt. This custom is based on the Rabbinical rendering of the Biblical passage "Thou shalt not seethe the kid in its mother's milk."[7]

The rules of the killing of animals among Jews and those governing the diet of Jews were no doubt prompted to a great extent by hygienic considerations.

These are the main ceremonial institutions of the Jews. There are a great many more of minor importance. To treat them all would be an almost interminable task. The descriptions given in the course of these chapters suffice to give a fair idea of those

[6] Gen. 32: 32.
[7] Ex 23: 19.

institutions practiced by most Jews in their
synagogues and homes, and of such institutions to which Jews are expected to conform
in the course of their religious life.

FINIS.

INDEX